DATE DUE

Purposes
of
Preaching

DATE DUE

ID0465566

Purposes of Preaching

JANA CHILDERS, ED.

CHALICE
PRESS
ST. LOUIS, MISSOURI

Cover art: © Fotosearch Stock Photography
Cover and interior design: Elizabeth Wright

This book is printed on acid-free, recycled paper.

Visit Chalice Press on the World Wide Web at
www.chalicepress.com

10 9 8 7 6 5 4 3 2 1   04 05 06 07 08 09

Library of Congress Cataloging-in-Publication Data

Purposes of preaching / Jana Childers, ed.
    p. cm.
Includes bibliographical references.
ISBN 0-8272-2997-6 (pbk. : alk. paper)
1. Preaching. I. Childers, Jana.
BV4211.3.P87 2004
251–dc22   2004002456

Printed in the United States of America

Contents

Contributors

Ronald J. Allen is the Nettie Sweeney and Hugh Th. Miller Professor of Preaching and Second Testament at Christian Theological Seminary in Indianapolis, Indiana.

Charles L. Campbell is associate professor of homiletics at Columbia Theological Seminary in Decatur, Georgia.

Jana Childers is dean of the seminary and professor of homiletics and speech-communication at San Francisco Theological Seminary in San Anselmo, California, and a minister in the Presbyterian Church (USA).

Teresa L. Fry Brown is associate professor of homiletics at Candler School of Theology in Atlanta, Georgia.

Lucy Lind Hogan is professor of preaching and worship at Wesley Theological Seminary in Washington, D.C., and a priest in the Episcopal Church.

John S. McClure is the Charles G. Finney Professor of Homiletics at the Divinity School of Vanderbilt University in Nashville, Tennessee.

Christine Smith is professor of preaching at United Theological Seminary of the Twin Cities in New Brighton, Minnesota.

Thomas H. Troeger is dean of academic affairs and the Ralph E. and Norma E. Peck Professor of Preaching and Communication at Iliff School of Theology in Denver, Colorado.

Mary Donovan Turner is the Carl Patton Associate Professor of Preaching at Pacific School of Religion in Berkeley, California, and a minister in the Christian Church (Disciples of Christ).

Paul Scott Wilson is professor of homiletics at Emmanuel College of Victoria University in the University of Toronto, Canada.

Preface

The working title of this volume, at least for some time and in my own mind, was *The Purpose of Preaching*. It's not that I thought that the ten contributing voices would achieve unanimity. Certainly, if anyone had asked me, I would have said I expected a nice range of diversity. That's why we selected the ten outstanding homileticians that we did. Chalice Press and I hoped that they would capture a snapshot of North American homiletics in the late twentieth and early twenty-first century. What we got, I am happy to say, is more than we bargained for.

In this collection of essays, leading scholars in the field of homiletics, all of them powerful preachers, pour their hearts out about the work to which they've given their lives. What is it about preaching that elicits such passion and commitment from its practitioners? What is it that gives it its peculiar power with listeners? Read on. Ten important answers to the question are collected here. We hope that the threads of difference and similarity that run among them will help spark a larger and longer conversation. With that in mind, we dedicate this volume to those from whom we've learned, especially Fred B. Craddock, Eugene L. Lowry, and Lucy Atkinson Rose, and to those who are coming along after us, in hopes that the conversation will continue to enlarge for generations to come.

Jana Childers
San Anselmo, California
Spring, 2004

1

Preaching as Mutual Critical Correlation through Conversation

RONALD J. ALLEN

The calling of the preacher is to help the congregation move toward a Christian interpretation of the world. The preacher wants to help the congregation learn to think, feel, and act from the perspective of the gospel. Week by week the cumulative effect of sermons should contribute to the congregation responding to the deepest questions of life. Who is God? From the perspective of the gospel, who are we as individuals and communities? How are we to understand the world? What does God offer? What does God ask? What are we to do to fulfill the divine purposes for us and for the world? Preaching is theological interpretation of life.

I join a number of other preachers and teachers of preaching by thinking of the sermon as a conversation in which congregation, preacher, and others search for an adequate theological interpretation of life in all its dimensions.[1] The content of the conversation is mutual critical correlation of Christian tradition with the contemporary setting.

Preaching as Conversation

By "conversation" I do not typically mean give-and-take, out loud, between the preacher and the congregation in the worship

1

space. Rather, the experience of preaching and hearing the sermon can have the qualities of a vibrant conversation. More than thirty years ago, Reuel Howe pointed out that a sermon spoken by a single person can have a dialogical character when the preacher "feels responsible for and responds to the patterns of experience and understanding" of the listeners, and when the community recognizes its own life and issues in the sermon.[2] The preaching conversation often involves voices in addition to the preacher and the congregation.

The preacher speaks in monologue, but the congregation feels as though they are participating in the sermon in a way similar to conversing around a dinner table.

> YOUTH: "We've got a big assignment at school."
> PARENT: "Oh, what's that?"
> YOUTH: *[Gives bare outline of assignment.]*
> *[Sibling surreptitiously tosses a pea at the Youth. Momentary laughter.]*
> FRIEND OF YOUTH STAYING FOR SUPPER: "I can't believe our teacher is asking us to do this project." *[Gives further details.]*
> PARENT: "Maybe you could ask your teacher about the rationale for this assignment."
> *[Thoughtful silence]*
> PARENT: "Hmm. How do you feel about this assignment?"
> *[Youth and Friend report feelings of curiosity, adventure, anxiety, and fear.]*
> FRIEND: "I've never thought of anything like this, and it's a little scary. I mean, what if we take it seriously?"
> GRANDPARENT: "Oh, I remember we had to do something like what you have to do when I was young in the days of Noah. *[Gets out family photo album. Tells story]*. I didn't like it, but it helped me and I lived to tell you about it."
> PARENT: "So, Youth, what do you need?"
> *[Youth and Friend begin to name things they need.]*
> SIBLING: "I have some of that stuff. If you promise to respect it, I'll loan it to you—that is, if your addled brain can handle it." *[Shoots pea at Youth but hits Friend.]*
> PARENT: "Speaking of respect *[looking at Sibling]*, we need to show respect for everyone at the table."
> COUSIN: "Your topic seems strange to you, but have you thought about how it might seem to people who don't have what you have?"

NEIGHBOR: *[popping into the kitchen to borrow sugar]:* "I heard something on National Public Radio about that just today. You can log on to their Web site and get a transcript."
[Phone call (during dinner, of course) for The Youth, who returns]
YOUTH: "Some kids are getting together at the library tonight to work on this project. We need to be there."
PARENT: "I suppose you'll need the car to go to the library."
YOUTH: "Yes, and when I had it earlier today, it was low on gas. The only thing lower is the amount of money in my pocket. Hint. Hint."

Although this vignette is stilted, it still reveals the essence of conversation, as identified by the contemporary philosopher Hans-Georg Gadamer. "A conversation is a process of...people understanding each other."[3] We usually think of conversations as verbal interchanges among people; however, we can also have conversations with written materials, artistic expressions, political and social events, or other phenomena. As in the interchange above, participants not only seek to understand one another but also to clarify values and anticipate courses of action.

According to Gadamer, "The first condition of the art of conversation is to ensure that the other person is with us."[4] Each participant must respect the otherness or integrity of all other participants.[5] We need to identify clearly and accurately what the others truly believe and do not believe, how they act and do not act. We are ethically obligated to listen to, and respect, the other. As Gadamer continues, in "true conversation" all participants open themselves to the others in interchange, considering the viewpoints and trying to understand the issue from the others' points of view.[6]

David Tracy, a leading systematic theologian at the University of Chicago, points out that the heart of conversation is questioning. We "learn to give in to the movement required by questions worth exploring." While we certainly take account of the points of view with which we start, "Neither my present opinions on the question nor the text's original response to the question, but the question itself, must control every conversation." Tracy stresses that a conversation "is not a confrontation. It is not a debate. It is not an exam. It is questioning itself. It is a willingness to follow the question wherever it may go. It is dialogue."[7]

Authentic conversation is not easy. Tracy points out that conversation has hard rules: Say only what you mean; say it as accurately as you can; listen to and respect what the other says, however different or other; be willing to correct or defend your opinions if challenged by the conversation partner; be willing to argue if necessary, to confront if demanded, to endure necessary conflict, to change your mind if the evidence suggests it.[8] When these rules hold sway, conversation is energetic–while sometimes difficult and occasionally painful–but nearly always important.

While the first rule is respect for the other, that does not mean all opinions turn out to be equally authoritative. Clark M. Williamson has written a systematic theology on a conversational model. He notes, "Lest one's mind become a garbage-heap of accumulated meanings deposited there by one's conversation partners, one must critically integrate these meanings with the values and perspectives that one brought to the conversation. Commitment to a more supreme and embracing good facilitates this kind of integration."[9] One of the purposes of conversation is to sort out those things that seem more and less promising.

A conversation often affects us. It may reinforce what we already think, feel, or do. It may prompt us to modify our thoughts and actions. It may introduce us to possibilities that are so generative and promising that we turn away from previous patterns of thought, emotion, and action and toward new ones. It may raise questions that we have not previously considered and about which we are not ready to make up our minds.

When the image of conversation is transferred to preaching, Justo and Catherine Gonzalez, church historians and theologians, point out that the preacher is not "a lone-ranger" but is a member of an interpreting *community*.[10] The conversation begins in sermon preparation as the preacher listens to others, and honors their otherness. The sermon itself has the ethos of a conversation in that the various conversation partners engage in honest, sensitive probing of questions related to life in Christian perspective.

The goal of the preaching conversation is to help the Christian community move toward a theologically adequate Christian interpretation of the world. From the standpoint of Christian vision, how should we evaluate and appropriate the past? How should we understand and live in the present? What should we plan for a future that will embody the gospel in personal and social reality?

Partners in the Preaching Conversation

Preachers often assume that the purpose of preaching is to offer an exposition of the significance of a biblical text for today's world.[11]

While I certainly affirm that preaching from biblical passages can be an important way to help the congregation interpret God and the world theologically, the motif of preaching as conversation suggests that the preparation and movement of the sermon could (and sometimes should) originate from other points and involve other voices.

The partners in the sermon conversation include not only the Bible (both individual passages and themes), but also elements of Christian history, doctrine, and practice; voices in the broader contemporary Christian community; and contributions from the wider world–personal and social situations and experiences, the arts, the social sciences, and the life of the preacher. A sermon could start from any of these points and involve several of these voices with the goal of helping the congregation move toward an adequate theological understanding of the text, topic, or situation.

In the case of each conversation partner, the preacher asks, "What does this partner ask us to believe is true of God? What does it ask us to accept as God's purposes for the world? What does it ask us to do?" The preacher and the congregation engage these partners through listening, questioning, critical reflection, and naming insight to determine the degree to which their interaction with each partner helps the community come to an understanding and behavior concerning God and the world.

Conversation takes place throughout the life of the sermon– from the time the preacher is thinking about the focus of the sermon through preparation and embodiment. Hopefully, the conversation continues in the hearts and minds of individuals and among community members after the preacher finishes speaking.

The *Bible* is one of the preacher's most consistent conversation partners. The Bible is not a single book but a library of interpretations of the presence and purposes of God from the perspective of different communities–e.g., Elohists, Yahwists, deuteronomists, priests, sages, apocalyptists, and Hellenistic Jewish communities. While the different biblical trajectories share important perspectives, they also put forward different nuances of understanding God and the world.

The sermon conversation usually focuses on one or two biblical passages; however, preachers can also develop sermons in dialogue with biblical themes–ideas or images that develop across several passages or books.[12] The pastor and people ask, "What does this passage or theme ask us to believe concerning God, the divine purposes for the world, and what we should do?"

The Bible is more than an ordinary voice in the preaching conversation. It has a proven record for helping communities in very different times and places come to clear and compelling senses of the presence and leading of God; however, congregations (and preachers) sometimes develop myopic views of scripture. While it is a primal theological guide, it is not imperial; selected passages and themes do not represent optimum understandings of God or the divine purposes for the world. Approaching the Bible conversationally encourages us to identify points at which the Bible is more and less helpful.

Contemporary sermons often leapfrog from the world of the Bible to today without taking into account the fact that Christians in the intervening millennia have often thought in very helpful ways about the subject of the sermon. *Christian history and tradition* are often potent partners in the preaching conversation. I think of Christian history and tradition as reaching from the time of the Bible to the present. This tradition is not a monolithic body of fixed and unchanging ideas, but like the Bible contains multiple voices who interpret Christian faith from the perspective of the worldviews and issues of their times and places. These voices include events, movements, theologians (e.g., Augustine, Calvin, Campbell) as well as official collective statements (e.g., Nicene Creed, Westminster Shorter Catechism). The preaching community has recently begun to listen to voices that the tradition has often marginalized. Clark Williamson points out that Christian tradition is constantly in the process of critically rethinking itself in light of new questions, information, and circumstances.[13] The sermon continues such conversations into the present.

While a pastor or congregation may sometimes be overwhelmed by the idea of bringing "Christian history and tradition" into a preaching conversation, a preacher can often ferret out a few voices that are particularly important to the congregation. These voices would ordinarily include the historic denomination of the congregation.

Contemporary theologians often contribute in an important way to the sermon. Such theologians try to help the church think afresh about the gospel and its implications for today. Theologians try to help congregations understand what is most important to believe about God, Christ, the Holy Spirit, the church, and the world; and help the community grasp how these things contribute to the shaping of personal and corporate life.[14] Contemporary theologians frequently speak from social locations that have not been prominent in previous generations–e.g., from the place of women in the social world, or those who are repressed by racism, or otherwise oppressed or abused. Theologians often help the church reinforce traditional teachings and actions, but sometimes they lead the church to reformulate and even reject aspects of the tradition when such aspects do not serve God's purposes.

Along this line, one of the most important impulses in contemporary theology is an emphasis on suspicion. We learn to ask of every biblical text or theme, every Christian teaching from history, Christian practice, and personal and social situation: Do voices in the conversation ask us to believe and act in ways that are contrary to the divine purposes?

The *congregation* seldom talks aloud as part of the message; however, John S. McClure, a leading thinker in contemporary preaching, points out that the preacher can involve the members of the congregation directly in the preparation of the sermon by creating a feed-forward group.[15] A small group of people meets with the preacher and talks about the text, doctrine, Christian practice, or personal or social situation that is the focus of the sermon. A pastor who does not meet with a feed-forward group sometimes imagines a group of people in the study during the preparation of the sermon. A minister may want to interview specific people in the congregation who are related to the subject of the sermon. Preachers can also ascertain congregational perspectives through everyday pastoral life– e.g., calling in hospitals and homes, committee meetings, encounters in the mall.

Voices from the *wider world* beyond the congregation and even the Christian community can also become a part of the sermon interchange. These voices can come from individual persons or from events and movements. I am often helped by listening to contemporary philosophy and the media (e.g., movies, talk shows); by the social and physical sciences (e.g., sociology, psychology); and by the arts. Each is a genuine other who may contribute insights, questions, experiences, and images to the conversation. While a pastor and people may initially feel inundated by the number of sources to whom they could listen, the preacher can often find a guide in the congregation or neighborhood (or on the Internet) who can help sort voices that are more and less promising.

The *life experience of the preacher* is a part of the sermon conversation whether or not the preacher is aware of it. Our experiences, our values, and our predispositions (conscious and unconscious) inevitably affect how we interpret God, congregation, and world. Preachers need to name and reflect critically on how their experience impinges upon the interpretation of the matters that are important to the preaching conversation. In the sermon itself, preachers can often speak from their own experience. Congregants often identify with the preacher's struggles, fears, and hopes.

God is omnipresent and, therefore, is involved in all phases of the sermon. As a relational (process) theologian, I do not believe that God tries to write the sermon word for word, but is present with the preacher and the congregation to try to lure the conversation to the optimum possibility for the community available when the sermon is preached. God is with the preacher and the people in the phase of preparation, urging them to be sensitive to the highest possibilities for helping the community to realize God's unconditional love and to respond to God's vision for a just world. During the sermon itself, God urges all to be open to the same insights. Of course, a minister or church may not perceive the divine leading, or may subvert or even reject it. In these latter cases, God works with the preacher, the sermon, and the congregation in order to make the most of the possibilities that result from the choices of the preacher and the congregation. God never gives up on a preacher, a sermon, or a congregation.

The Preaching Conversation as Mutual Critical Correlation

The preaching conversation seeks a mutual critical correlation between claims of Christian tradition from the past (or from other communities in the present) and the congregation in its present time, place, and social-intellectual-theological location. The notion of correlation received its most famous relatively recent explication in the *Systematic Theology* of Paul Tillich. The preacher attempts to correlate what people believed to be true in the past (or in other locations) with what the preacher's current congregation-community believes to be true. This approach recognizes that all human awareness and expression contains elements of interpretation that are tied to the worldview and other assumptions in each historical era. People in different situations may use different language to talk about similar experiences and phenomena. Tillich sought to correlate the questions and issues of contemporary people with elements of Christian tradition to show how the tradition addressed such questions and issues. The preacher's primary task is to interpret contemporary questions in such a way that the tradition can answer them and vice versa.[16]

For instance, in one of the most famous sermons of the twentieth century, "You are Accepted," Tillich identifies the yearning for acceptance as one of the primary yearnings of persons living in mid- to late-twentieth-century North America.[17] Tillich correlates grace (unmerited favor) with acceptance. The experience of unmerited acceptance by a power greater than the human being is a contemporary correlate of the experience of grace. In order for their yearning to be put to rest, people need to accept the fact that they are accepted.

Preachers sometimes refer to this approach (and others similar to it) as building a bridge from the ancient text to the contemporary world. This way of thinking assumes that the preacher can always find a positive meaning in the ancient source that will strengthen the congregation's perception of the gospel and witness to it.

One of Tillich's perceptive students, David Tracy, saw problems in Tillich's approach, however.[18] The correlation largely went one way: The present raised the question or the issue while the tradition supplied the answer. Tracy observes that the tradition often criticizes aspects of life in the present, and calls for repentance and for reformulating current beliefs and actions to bring them more fully into accord with the gospel. Furthermore, Tillich's approach assumes the trustworthiness of the tradition. Tracy, however, notes that insights and issues from the contemporary world can raise questions about the adequacy of affirmations and prescriptions for action in the tradition.

The preacher, then, is called to mutual critical correlation.[19] The preacher not only identifies today's questions to which the tradition gives answer, but also criticizes the contemporary world from the perspective of the gospel; at the same time, the preacher criticizes the Christian tradition from the perspective of contemporary insights and experiences. As a result of the practice of mutual critical correlation, the congregation must also reevaluate and even reformulate aspects of its interpretation of the gospel

For instance, the biblical world generally assumes the validity of patriarchy and slavery. By contrast, many contemporary people recognize that patriarchy and slavery are oppressive, abusive, and even violent. Patriarchy and slavery go against the grain of the gospel with its assurance of God's love for all and God's will for justice for all. They institutionalize injustice. The church, then, must criticize these aspects of the tradition if its witness to the gospel is to be adequate.

Preachers do not assume that they can build a positive bridge from the past to the present. Before building a bridge, preacher and community engage in a conversation with the various partners in the congregation to determine whether voices from the past can directly strengthen today's community.

Criteria for Mutual Critical Correlation

Clark Williamson points out that in order to practice mutual critical correlation, the church must have norms by which to gauge the adequacy of both Christian tradition and contemporary experience.[20] To pick up an earlier example, the preacher needs to have norms by which to say that the experience of acceptance is equivalent to the experience of grace. The church needs to be able to say why patriarchy and slavery are inadequate. Toward this end, Williamson proposes three criteria intended to distill the core of Christian witness: appropriateness to the gospel, intelligibility, and moral plausibility.

The preacher asks, "What does an element of Christian tradition (e.g., a passage from the Bible, a doctrine, a Christian practice, or other Christian witness) ask me to believe and do? Is that appropriate to the gospel, intelligible, and morally plausible?"[21] The preacher also asks, "What does an element of contemporary thinking and experience (e.g., a personal or social event, or a perspective, value, or behavior) ask me to believe and do? Is it appropriate to the gospel, intelligible, morally plausible?"

1. *Appropriateness to the gospel.* The preacher aims to help the church determine the degree to which every voice in the sermon conversation—e.g., a biblical passage or theme, an element of doctrine and practice, ethical prescriptions, feelings, personal and social circumstances—is appropriate to (or consistent with) the gospel. Following Williamson, I take the gospel to be the news (revealed through Israel and confirmed for the church through Jesus Christ) of the promise of God's unconditional love for each and every created entity and the call of God for justice (that is relationships of love and abundance) for each and all. The preacher asks of each partner in the preaching conversation, "Is this text, etc., appropriate to the news of God's unconditional love promised to each and all, and God's call for justice?"

Williamson points out why this criterion is crucial. "The church lives by and from the proclamation of the gospel." The only reason the church exists is to alert the world to the presence and implications of the good news. "The church claims to be proclaiming the gospel." The norm of appropriateness "asks whether this is really so. The church can be so eager to be popular and accepted, or so zealous to be contextualized in a given culture or ethos, that it forgets that the word it is given to proclaim transcends and criticizes all cultures as it also calls for being critically contextualized in them. We are always in danger in the church of running amok with our latest cliché."[22]

Most passages from the Bible or other elements of Christian tradition are appropriate to the gospel. For instance, Isaiah 42:1–9, the first of four servant songs in Isaiah, describes Israel as a "light to the nations." The life of Israel is to be a model (a light) to the gentile peoples of God's steadfast love and of how God wants all peoples to live so that they may be blessed. This hope is consistent with the news of God's love for all and of God's will for justice for all. The preaching conversation might explore how today's congregation can model God's love and justice in the early twenty-first century.

Occasional elements of Christian tradition, however, deny that God loves some people or that God wills justice for some people or communities. John 8:39–47 denies that certain Jewish people are children of Sarah and Abraham but are, instead, descendents of the devil. This text denies God's love for these people. The sermon conversation needs to name the theological inadequacy of this text and expose its ideological (anti-Jewish) bias.

2. *Intelligibility.* The sermon needs to ask the congregation to believe and do things that are intelligible in the contemporary world. As Williamson pungently says, "The simplest defense of the criterion of intelligibility is to point out that there is no alternative to it other than incoherence and meaninglessness."[23] This criterion has three dimensions.

(a) The content of the sermon must be *clear enough for people to understand it.* The congregation must understand what the preacher says so that they can enter into the conversation. The preacher needs not only to use clear language, but must sometimes provide basic information about aspects of the biblical text or other elements of Christian tradition. For example, when the book of Hebrews says that Christ is a priest according to the order of Melchizedek (4:14–5:10), the preacher needs not only to pronounce Melchizedek correctly but also to explain what it means to call Christ a priest in that order.

(b) The preaching conversation must come to a conclusion that is *logically consistent* with other affirmations and actions that the church accepts and does. "Preachers who do not have some systematic, coherent way" of making sense of the diversity of sacred scripture, Christian doctrine and practice, and the wider Christian world can easily "proclaim messages that contradict and undercut one another. If preachers are blown this way and that by every wind of thought and feeling that comes along, indeed, by diverse texts from week to week, what will happen to their hearers?"[24] Of course, this norm assumes the criterion of appropriateness to the gospel: to be logically consistent within the Christian house, elements of tradition and contemporary experience must be consistent with the gospel.

For instance, Psalm 105 celebrates divine *hesed* (God's steadfast love) for Israel. In the process of celebrating God's steadfast love for Israel, however, the Psalm claims that God carried out multiple acts of violence on the Egyptians including fouling their water and destroying their supply of fish there by turning their river to blood, inflicting them with painful and debilitating plagues, sending hunger throughout the land by causing famine, striking their firstborn dead, and drowning the Egyptian army in the sea. While such actions liberated Israel from slavery, they are not logically consistent with the idea that God loves *all* and wills justice for *all.*

Diversity and difference in the Christian house do not always mean contradiction. The Christian tradition, for instance, contains several different understandings of salvation ranging from unmediated access to God in the heavenly world to political, social, and economic liberation. While these views differ from one another, they seldom contradict. They represent different ways of understanding salvation in different historical moments and contexts.

(c) The sermon must be *believable.*[25] David Kelsey, a well-known theologian, says that a claim must be "seriously imaginable."[26] The sermon can ask us only to believe and do things that make sense given how people in today's world interpret the world and its operation. "It is important to observe that in being concerned with intelligibility, we are not importing into the [Christian] tradition something from outside it. A living tradition is always concerned with intelligibility, with 'making sense' of the situation and the inheritance of faith." Indeed, "that the scriptures themselves represent a process of reinterpretation through five major cultural epochs itself testifies to the fact that the biblical tradition persistently sought to 'make sense' of itself in new situations, as well as to make sense of new situations in the light of its legacy of faith."[27]

Preacher and congregation need to handle this norm carefully. On one hand, the preaching conversation should seek an interpretation of a biblical text, theme, doctrine, practice, or experience that does not ask the community to suspend what it otherwise believes to be true. In the latter case, the claim of the sermon becomes unintelligible and unbelievable. Such preaching undermines the credibility of the Christian community. For example, 2 Kings 4:1–7 tells the story of God providing an unending supply of oil for a needy widow through the prophet Elisha. Few residents of contemporary North America seriously imagine that God could miraculously fill our vessels with oil. Furthermore, if God could help needy people by intervening in the world in such a direct way, but does not, then is God truly trustworthy?

On the other hand, the sermon conversation may need to consider the possibility that a biblical text or some other element from Christian tradition invites us to enlarge or reframe our understanding of how God works in the world or how we can respond. Preachers and congregants are finite. Our perception is often too limited. At the surface level, we may not believe that God literally fills the jugs of needy widows. At a deeper level, the story may speak figuratively of God making provision.

3. *Moral plausibility.* Does the element of Christian tradition that is the focus of the sermon invite the community to believe and do things that are morally plausible, that is, to treat all persons as beloved of God and with justice? This criterion makes explicit an aspect of the criterion of appropriateness to the gospel. Clark Williamson shows the immediate and urgent practicality of this criterion.

Frequently there is in the text itself an attitude toward, e.g., women, or Jews, or slavery which simply must be rejected by any Christian who even remotely tries to live a Christian life. After hundreds of years of experience with slavery in this country and apartheid in South Africa, after thousands of years of anti-Judaism, of pogroms and Holocaust, after millennia of the oppression of women, one must simply say no to all attitudes from the past that would justify and reinforce such prejudices today.[28] While Williamson particularly has biblical passages in view, his point applies to Christian doctrines, writings, practices, and behaviors. The sermon conversation can also consider values and behaviors in the contemporary culture from the perspective of this criterion. Of course, the preacher must do more than say no to injustices. Minister and sermon must show how the congregation and the wider community can move toward embodying divine love for all and can facilitate justice for all.

Preacher and congregation can sometimes make a distinction between the *surface* and *deeper* meanings of a text or other aspect of Christian witness that helps the community find positive significance in a witness that is troubling (theologically, intellectually, or morally). The surface meaning is the plain meaning of what a text asks us to believe or do in the language, imagery, presuppositions, and worldview of its culture. That dimension of the text may be troubling. The deeper meaning is dimensions of the text that are not limited to particular cultural associations. The deeper point of a text or doctrine often has abiding significance. Elements of experience in the ancient and contemporary settings are often similar but go by different names. Through conversation, preacher and congregation explore points of deeper contact.

For instance, Isaiah pleads to God, "O that you would tear open the heavens and come down," and manifest justice in the world (64:1). On the surface, Isaiah assumes a three-story universe. The upper story is heaven, where God dwells, and is separated from the middle story (earth) by a dome. Isaiah asks God to rip a hole in the dome and literally climb down from the upper story. Few people today accept this cosmology. However, at a deeper level, Isaiah asks for God to work toward manifesting justice in the present world. The preaching conversation might explore how today's community can understand God to be at work in the world for justice.

Moments in the Preaching Conversation

I think of the preaching conversation emerging in moments. For convenience of discussion, I list these phases in a linear sequence. Sometimes these moments occur in the order that follows. In actual practice, they often take place in much different sequences. Sometimes multiple moments occur simultaneously.

The first moment in the movement of a preaching conversation is to identify the focus of the sermon.[29] As I have already indicated, this subject is usually suggested by the community's encounter with one more of the following: a biblical text or theme; a Christian doctrine or other element of Christian history or tradition (e.g., an affirmation of faith, a day in the church year such as Pentecost, a particular figure or event); a perspective from Christian practice (e.g., prayer); a perspective from systematic theology; or a personal or social experience.

The second moment is for preacher and community to name their pre-understandings of the focus. Pastor and people name the naïve and often uncritical perspectives that they bring to the conversation. This phase is important so that these nascent inclinations will not inappropriately preform the conversation. The preacher can help the members of the community (including the preacher) list and describe their preexisting viewpoints and experiences. This moment in the preaching conversation may bring to the surface points and associations that are unsettled, points at which minister and flock are in need of further information or perspective, or points at which the community has limited or atypical experience.[30] Such pre-associations often reflect the social location of the preacher and the congregation. When these pre-understandings are named, the minister and congregation can take them into account and reflect critically on them and bring them into the sermon. The hermeneutic of suspicion is often of particular illumination in this phase.[31]

The third moment is to listen to the various others in the preaching conversation–the Bible, representatives from history and tradition, theologians, the members of the congregation, voices from the wider world, and the preacher's own life. This moment includes exegesis of biblical passages and themes, taking account of the historical settings of partners from other times and places, analyzing the contexts of contemporary voices, and looking into one's own heart and life with honesty. These participants will raise questions, alert the community to necessary information, share feelings, state preferences, articulate why they believe and do certain things (and why not others), and describe behaviors that accompany the focus of the preaching conversation. The preacher will often listen to written texts (e.g., the Bible, voices from history), but will sometimes speak directly with people (e.g., personal interviews or through a collaborative conversation, as described by John McClure, between pastor and a small group of people) or review (or imagine) how the subject of the conversation relates to various members of the community, or have another kind of experience in the medium of the partner (e.g., watching a movie, viewing a painting).

Both John McClure and Lucy Rose use the image of a round table in the midst of their discussions of preaching as conversation.[32] During this phase of sermon preparation, I sometimes find it helpful to take this visual clue and draw a round table with each participant in the conversation in a separate seat. I then draw lines that show how the different participants in the congregation interact with one another. Others frequently help us see things that we may not catch in biblical passages and themes; in persons, events, and doctrines from Christian history; in Christian practices; in personal and social situations, and experiences in our own lives.

The initial three moments perform the indispensable function of listening to the others in the conversation voice their own perceptions. The fourth phase is the heart of the preaching conversation: identifying interpretive possibilities and engaging in mutual critical correlation among the multiple voices. Preacher and congregation compare and contrast the various interpretations with one another in light of the criteria of appropriateness to the gospel, intelligibility, and moral plausibility, and decide which one(s) make the most sense.

One of the most penetrating insights of contemporary philosophy and theology is that all human awareness contains elements of interpretation. We never achieve completely pure, objective understanding. David Tracy eloquently summarizes an implication of this insight for preaching.

> If one demands certainty, one is assured of failure. We can
> never possess absolute certainty. But we can achieve a good–
> that is, a relatively adequate–interpretation: relative to the
> power of disclosure and concealment of the text, relative to
> the skills and attentiveness of the interpreter, relative to the
> kind of conversation possible for the interpreter in a particular
> culture at a particular time.[33]

A specific sermon is seldom the last word of a preacher and congregation on a subject. A sermon is a mile-marker that indicates where the community's capacity for discernment has led them at a particular moment in history. Later, minister and congregation may look back on that sermon and rethink its conclusion from the perspective of fresher insights.

The idea of the sermon as an *interpretation* of the gospel emerging from the give-and-take of conversation and resulting in a *relatively adequate witness* may seem thin to preachers who are accustomed to thinking of the sermon as "the word of God." To such preachers, I maintain that I am only making explicit aspects of preaching that are sometimes implicit or even hidden. Even preachers who believe that the words of the Bible and the words of the preacher are, syllable by syllable, God's words must take account of the fact that persons in the church disagree about how best to interpret the Bible and Christian doctrine and practice. Biblical scholars have made a holy industry of different interpretations, as have church historians and theologians. Preachers interpret when they prefer the opinion of one scholar to the opinion of another. I am simply trying to put the interpretive dimensions of preaching on the table for critical reflection.

Preaching conversations that are pursued straightforwardly with depth, imagination, and rigor will usually come to a "good enough" interpretive possibility. Some preaching dialogues, however, may not arrive at resolution. The community may not come to clarity. In such cases, preacher and people may need to agree to continue the conversation. Borrowing an image from the computer world, the minister and flock may need to "keep the file open." At such times, the congregation may need to live in ambiguity while recognizing that God is with them as they pursue further insight.

This conversational approach to interpretation has certain dangers. The participants may be thoughtless, hurtful, self-serving, and idolatrous. The preacher or the people may confuse a majority opinion with a satisfactory mutual critical correlation. A congregation that cannot come to consensus may too quickly use that irresolution as an excuse to put the issue aside. The pastor needs to be aware that a congregational consensus may be so mistaken that the optimum contribution a sermon may make in the ongoing dialogue is to go against the community's prevailing view.

General Directions in the Preaching Conversation

A preaching conversation usually results in a pastor and community coming to one of three possible interpretive directions.

The sermon can *run with the text, doctrine, practice, or situation.* The subject of the sermon is appropriate to the gospel, intelligible, and morally plausible. The sermon may need to explain (through exegesis, historical recollection, or contemporary reflection) elements of the subject of the sermon so that all in the congregation have a sufficient grasp of them. The main work of the sermon itself, however, is to help the community identify these positive possibilities and how to respond to them.

The preaching conversation may *recognize elements in the subject of the sermon that contribute positively to the world of the congregation as well as aspects that are problematic.* When I was preaching every week as the minister of a congregation, this relationship was the most frequent between the subject of the sermon and our community. This case usually comes about when a text, historical witness, theological voice, practice, or situation appears on the surface to be unintelligible. Moving deeper, however, shows that the subject of the sermon does contain elements that are intelligible. When preacher and congregants are theologically alert, this path can sometimes lead the community to identify a positive message in some materials, practices, and experiences whose surface meaning appears to be inappropriate to the gospel or morally implausible. The preaching conversation helps the Christian community retrieve the deep dimensions of the text and apply them to the local situation.

The preaching conversation can *take issue with the focus of the sermon.* People and pastor may disagree with what the text, historical voice, theological witness, practice, or situation asks them to believe or do. The preaching conversation takes this turn when the material or experience that is the subject of the sermon is fundamentally inappropriate to the gospel or morally implausible. Few congregations are accustomed to learning that aspects of Christian tradition are mistaken. My experience when preaching in this mode is that some in the congregation are relieved. I remember a woman who burst out, "I wanted to believe your way for a long time, but I didn't know I could and still be a Christian." Some members of the community, however, will be nervous and even hostile about this direction. When the preaching conversation disagrees with a text or other element of Christian life, preacher and people are advised to do so in a gentle and probing way and to avoid being cavalier or inflammatory. The conversation in the sermon itself can carefully and patiently explain the point at disagreement and offer an alternative theological vision. As someone asked me during a Bible study, "If I can't believe that God wants us to dash the babies of our enemies against the rocks [in reference to Psalm 137], what can I believe?"

What about the Form of the Sermon?

For the last thirty years, the subject of the form of the sermon has been at the center of the preaching community. Scholars and preachers use the word *form* to refer to the shape, structure, movement, genre, pattern of organization, or outline of the sermon. Preaching classes usually encourage preachers to find their own styles and voices through which to bring the sermon to life. Preachers often spend quite a bit of time mulling over whether to use (or adapt) a stock sermon form, or whether to create a form for the sermon much as an author writes a novel.

The anthology *Patterns of Preaching: A Sermon Sampler* describes thirty different approaches to preaching and illustrates each with a sermon from a different recognized preacher.[34] For example, this collection summarizes the Puritan Plain Style (beginning, exegesis, theological reflection, application); Henry Mitchell's sermon as a journey to celebration, preaching verse by verse; Eugene Lowry's five-step "loop" (oops, ugh, aha, whee, yeah); Paul Scott Wilson's "four pages of the sermon"; David Buttrick's "plot and moves." Students assigned this book sometimes exclaim, "I didn't know there are thirty-four ways to preach," to which an instructor can only reply, "These thirty-four are just the beginning of the range of possibilities." *Patterns of Preaching*, for instance, does not mention sermon as midrash (an interpretive possibility from the tradition), or the new modes of preaching as testimony and preaching as confession.

The idea of preaching as conversation does not dictate a specific structure for the sermon. There is no uniform pattern for preaching as conversation. The conversational approach to the sermon is more a matter of ethos, spirit, or purpose than of outline. Such a sermon is marked by the qualities of careful listening to others, questioning, being questioned by them, identifying and assessing interpretive options, and moving toward as much consensus as the interpretive conversation will allow. Almost any sermonic form can manifest such characteristics, though some forms of preaching are more congenial to these purposes than others.

A few remarks on form may nonetheless help the reader who is wondering, "How do I take the thoughts, questions, images, and insights that emerge from the give-and-take of interaction with texts, people, and experiences, and put them together for a sermon that has a conversational character?"

At times a preacher can select a stock sermon form (e.g., Ricoeur's movement from first naiveté through critical reflection to second naiveté). At other times, a preacher may approach this phase of the life of the sermon after the model of an author creating a novel (as presented below). Sometimes I start with a definite movement in mind for the sermon, only to find that the sermon evolves unexpectedly. As a preacher, I find four approaches to the structure of the sermon regularly serve my own efforts to help the sermon itself take on a conversational quality.

Frequently the sermon develops *as an author creates a novel*.[35] When an author starts a novel, that writer usually has several things in mind—settings, characters, tensions, symbols and associations, and a broad outline for the plot. The characters develop almost as if they have a life of their own. Although the fingers of the writer create the characters on the screen (or on paper), the author frequently finds the characters saying and doing things that the author did not intend and did not imagine when the writing began. Similarly, I often begin to formulate the sermon itself with a question or issue, exegetical background, contributions from theologians (historical and contemporary), contemporary experience (including my own) with the focus of the sermon, scenes from novels or movies, and other materials. I have an inkling of where to begin the sermon as well as a general sense of the flow of the sermon. As I work, the sermon sort of emerges—sometimes quickly and easily, but frequently through struggle. The process of formalizing the sermon itself has similarities with a good conversation. The message sometimes takes very different turns than I had originally imagined.

A sermon can follow Paul Ricoeur's movement from first naiveté through critical reflection to second naiveté.[36] In first naiveté, preacher and community listen to the text or other focus of the sermon on its own terms. They ask, "What does the task ask us to believe or do?" In the phase of critical reflection, preacher and people note both the difficulties they have believing and doing as the text recommends, and reasons they can name that compel them to take the text seriously. For instance, the conversation might discover that a text contains mythological elements that we no longer believe. In the moment of second naiveté, the preaching conversation encourages the community to return to the text with a mature, critical perception of its difficulties while being willing to let the text name the world in ways that are appropriate to the gospel, intelligible, and morally credible. Preacher and community, for instance, might use mythological symbols from the text to speak figuratively of the congregation's experience in the world. Or the preaching conversation might diminish the element of naiveté in the third phase by stating unambiguously and nonmythologically what a congregation can believe and do.

Fred Craddock suggests that the preacher might *recreate in the pulpit the earlier phases of the preaching conversation.*[37] The preacher uses the various steps and moments in the prior phases of the preaching conversation as the outline for the sermon itself. By recreating the earlier moments of the preaching conversation in the presence of the congregation, the preacher invites the congregation to join in listening to the many voices in the exploration—questioning, probing, researching, reflecting, storytelling. Of course, for the sermon itself the preacher must greatly condense the several hours that went into the prior phases of conversation to the length of time that the typical congregation allows for the sermon.

The Wesleyan quadrilateral—a model for theological reflection—can easily be adapted to preaching.[38] The underlying premise of the quadrilateral is that the Christian community listens to four sources and their interaction to discern theologically how to interpret aspects of Christian life and witness. These four sources and their interworking can easily provide the outline for a sermon. In each case, minister and congregants seek to listen to the source in its otherness. First, the community asks what the Bible asks us to believe and do. Scholars in the Wesleyan tradition often stress that the Bible is not simply one source alongside others, but that it has a privileged (though not dictatorial) place. The second source is Christian tradition. What do important voices in the Christian past ask us to believe and do? The third source is experience. The conversation needs to help us name and analyze our experience of the subject of the sermon. What does our experience suggest we might say and do? Reason is the fourth source. Through reason we bring the other sources into interaction with one another, and we bring them into interaction with how we understand the world today. This step seeks to answer the question, "What makes sense for us to believe and do today?"

Conclusion

I close with a reminder that the sermon conversation should help the congregation encounter good news from God. Indeed, the word *gospel* translates a Greek word, *euangellion,* that means "good news." To be sure, preacher and people must confront their complicity in sin and evil, and must repent. We must sometimes come face to face with some very sorry things about our world and ourselves. Christian preaching, however, ultimately aims to help the community recognize and respond positively to the message of God's love for all and God's will for justice for all. Key questions to ask of every sermon are, "What is the good news in this sermon? For whom? How will it help them (us) experience and embody God's love and God's will for justice?"

More than fifty years ago, Russell Dicks, a professor of pastoral care, described conversation between pastor and parishioner as sacramental because, through conversation, the grace of God comes to expression.[39] While Dicks had in mind the relationships of pastor and individual persons, the point can extend to the sermon in the context of the congregational community. The preaching conversation can be sacramental, for the grace of God can pulse afresh throughout the conversation.

2

Resisting the Powers

CHARLES L. CAMPBELL

"When the unclean spirit has gone out of a person, it wanders through waterless regions looking for a resting place, but it finds none. Then it says, 'I will return to my house from which I came.' When it comes, it finds it empty, swept, and put in order. Then it goes and brings along seven other spirits more evil than itself, and they enter and live there; and the last state of that person is worse than the first. So will it be also with this evil generation."

While he was still speaking to the crowds, his mother and his brothers were standing outside, wanting to speak to him. Someone told him, "Look, your mother and your brothers are standing outside, wanting to speak to you." But to the one who had told him this, Jesus replied, "Who is my mother, and who are my brothers?" And pointing to his disciples, he said, "Here are my mother and my brothers! For whoever does the will of my Father in heaven is my brother and sister and mother."

(MATTHEW 12:43–50)

This text, so obscure at points, may seem like an odd place to begin some reflections on the purpose of preaching. Although Jesus is "speaking to the crowds," possibly preaching to them, the text

23

says nothing directly about preaching itself. Nor is it a text, with its mysterious reference to spirits "wandering through the waterless regions," that seems very pertinent to contemporary, mainline preachers. In the sermons I listen to, I don't hear much about demonic possession or the world of the spirits. Such topics just don't seem relevant to most sophisticated, twenty-first century congregations.

I want to suggest nevertheless that this text–or better, the juxtaposition of these two pericopes–sheds important light on the purpose of preaching in the contemporary church. In the first place, the text concludes with Jesus' emphasis on the community of faith that does God's will. That's where his address to the crowds leads– to an affirmation of the community that practices the way of God in the world. And that, I think, is the ultimate purpose of our preaching; that is the goal toward which our proclamation leads: the building up of the community of faith as a people who practice the way of God, as embodied in Jesus Christ, in and for the world.

As the larger context of Jesus' words about his true family makes clear, however, this community that does God's will must be built up in the midst of a world in which demonic powers assault people from every imaginable angle and seek to take them captive. Jesus' assertion about the community of faith occurs at the end of a series of exorcisms and a lengthy discussion about Jesus' engagement with the demonic powers in the world (see the remainder of Matthew 12). In building up the community of faith, Jesus must constantly resist these powers with the Word–performing exorcisms in order to set people free *from* the powers of death and *for* the way of life. And through his rather mysterious teaching in Matthew 12:43–45, Jesus suggests some directions for preachers who would build up the church in the midst of the demonic powers that assault the community of believers in countless ways.

Such preaching, the text suggests, requires a twofold movement. First of all, the preacher will need to exorcise the powers of death that hold people and churches captive, and prevent them from following the way of Jesus. Through such homiletical exorcisms, the preacher seeks to set people free from their captivity to the powers. Simply setting the church free *from* the powers, however, is not enough. For, as Jesus suggests, the assault of the powers is relentless; once "cast out" the demonic powers redouble their efforts to capture those who have been set free (vv. 44–45). Consequently, the second movement in such preaching involves building up the community in the practices of discipleship that will enable them to continue to resist the powers of death and live as God's people in and for the world. The preacher cannot simply "cast out" the demons and leave the church with an "empty" freedom (v. 44). Rather, the old practices shaped by the powers must be replaced with the practices of the new creation. This twofold movement can provide helpful direction to contemporary preachers who seek to build up the church in the face of the powers of death.[1]

Preaching as Exorcism

For the past few years I have been wrestling with a comment about preaching that Martin Luther made in his commentary on Isaiah: "[H]ow difficult an occupation preaching is. Indeed, to preach the Word of God is nothing less than to bring upon oneself all the furies of hell and of Satan, and therefore also of…every power of this world. It is the most dangerous kind of life to throw oneself in the way of Satan's many teeth."[2] For many contemporary preachers, this assertion may seem a bit strange and overly dramatic. Many of us, myself included, don't often think of the sermon as a life-and-death encounter with demonic powers. And our experience of sermons–whether as preachers or congregants–usually doesn't seem as dangerous or invigorating as Luther suggests. At times, after preaching a sermon or listening to one, we might find ourselves wishing that we *had* encountered one of Satan's many teeth; it might have livened things up a bit. Luther's words may seem rather extreme to many of us.

Jesus, however, probably would have understood Luther. When he speaks, Jesus regularly finds himself confronted by demonic powers. And through his words, he regularly challenges and casts out the powers of death that oppose his way. In the gospel of Luke, for example, Jesus' first three experiences of preaching bring him face to face with the demonic. Jesus' first experience of preaching–his basic preaching course–takes place out in the wilderness where, all alone, he must encounter the devil with nothing but the word of God (Lk. 4:1–13). To say the least, Jesus receives an invigorating introduction to the practice of preaching. He has to choose the right text and speak the appropriate word for the situation. And he has to do it three times in rapid succession. And his very life and mission depend on the word he proclaims. (He chooses, by the way, to do a sermon series from Deuteronomy.) Welcome to Preaching 101.

Jesus gets a tough introduction to homiletics. This is not the way I teach the introductory course in preaching at Columbia Seminary.

I do not send students into the wilderness by themselves to encounter the devil and preach the word of God as if their very lives depended on it. My approach is much more tame and pastoral. Students preach to supportive classmates in the familiar surroundings of the seminary chapel, where demons no doubt lurk but are rarely called forth. And after students preach, we try to buoy them up with plenty of positive feedback before turning to critique. Jesus' experience in the wilderness seems pretty foreign. But maybe Jesus' experience has something to teach us about the way we learn to preach. Maybe Jesus' encounter with the devil in the wilderness really is the paradigmatic preaching situation with which all preachers must grapple.

Following his introduction to preaching in the wilderness, Jesus, like many seminary students, goes off to preach in his home church in Nazareth (Lk. 4:16–30). Everything goes well at first. The congregation is amazed at the quality of Jesus' sermon. The hometown boy has seemingly made good (v. 22). Jesus' experience, however, doesn't conclude with smiling people filing out the door and telling him how wonderful he is. Instead, when Jesus challenges the powers of death implicit in religious exclusivism (vv. 23–27), a demonic mob spirit takes over the congregation, and the people seek to throw Jesus off a cliff. Jesus discovers, in Martin Luther's words, that preaching is a "most dangerous kind of life." Once again, Jesus' words directly confront (indeed call forth!) the demonic powers of the world that hold people captive to the ways of death.

Finally, following his experience in Nazareth, Jesus gets his first real, independent preaching "gig." He is no longer at seminary or in his home church. Instead, he enters the synagogue in Capernaum and begins to speak—and he does so with authority (Lk. 4:31–37). And here again, he is immediately confronted by "a man who had the spirit of an unclean demon" (v. 33). Jesus' preaching calls forth the demonic powers of the world to challenge him. And in Capernaum, in his first experience of preaching outside his home church, preaching and exorcism become intimately linked. Jesus' preaching calls forth the demonic powers, and then with a word Jesus casts out those powers.

Maybe Luther got it right. Maybe preaching really is a dramatic encounter with the demonic powers of the world. Maybe we should consider a central purpose of preaching to be *exorcism*. It at least sounds exciting. And, in fact, don't many people in our congregations deep down actually ache for a kind of exorcism? Don't many folks–preachers included—long to be set free from powers of death that have us in their grip and won't let us go—powers from which we cannot seem to free ourselves no matter how hard we try? After all, this is the key characteristic of demonic possession: We are no longer agents of our own lives, but go through the deadly motions dictated to us by the powers of the world that hold us captive—that "possess" us. And we need a word from beyond ourselves to set us free from our captivity.

Isn't that the situation of many in our churches? Maybe that's even our own situation as preachers. I don't come across too many people in churches who are intentionally evil and malevolent. I don't meet too many people who actively and consciously choose to sin and do harm. Very few, if any, leave the church saying, "Okay, that's over. Now I'm going to go out and do some serious sinning, some real evil." Rather, the people I meet are more like the person in the synagogue, who is possessed by something bigger and more powerful than himself, so much so that his words and actions are not really his own, but those of the demon that possesses him.

I talk to a lot of people like that—people who sense they are not really living, but can't do anything about it. "This is not life, but I can't seem to find an alternative." I feel that way myself much of the time. Indeed, most of us have some sense of the powers that hold us captive. We're told, for example, that consumption is the way of life. So, many of us consume and consume and consume, even though deep down we sense it is killing us and we know it is killing others, from the homeless people on our streets to the children who work in sweat shops around the globe. But we can't seem to stop. It's as if we're possessed. We're told that staying busy gives life meaning and purpose—not to mention giving us the money we need to consume. But now busyness has become a way of life—or, better, a way of death. People I talk to hate the busyness; they hate their overloaded date books and personal digital assistants. But they seem powerless to stop. It's as if they're possessed. People in our churches know the feeling of being caught in something larger and more powerful than themselves, something that seems to control their lives; they know what it means to be captive to the powers of death.

And they know it not just in their personal lives, but also in the face of the enormous problems in the world, before which they often feel powerless. Almost no one, for example, really wants homeless people living on the streets, but we can't seem to do anything to change it, and the number of homeless people just keeps on growing.

Almost no one really desires for children to be starving all over the globe, but the cemeteries continue to fill with those small bodies. And few people really wish for more violence, but kids keep killing kids, we can't control guns, and we are unable even to imagine alternatives to war. So, people often lose energy. They give up. They go along. And finally, they just give in to those powers that overwhelm them at every turn. And who can blame them? Who can blame us? It's a lot easier that way. It takes much less energy.

As preachers, the challenge we face, as William Stringfellow puts it, is not so much evil minds as paralyzed consciences. The problem is not so much malevolence as the *demoralization* of people "who have become captive and immobilized as human beings by their habitual obeisance to institutions or other principalities as idols."[3] On Sunday mornings, that is, most preachers do not face people who actively seek to do evil, but rather people who are complicit with the powers that hold them captive. In fact, in many instances these people are deeply frustrated by their complicity because they know the way they are following is not the way of life. Within this context, sin primarily involves complicity in our own moral death; it is the human inability or refusal to step into the freedom and life made possible in Jesus Christ, and enacted in baptism. The problem is as much *weakness* or *powerlessness* as active evil. It is, in short, a kind of possession.

And that suggests to me that in our time preaching once again needs to be a kind of exorcism. As Walter Wink notes, "Exorcism in its New Testament context is the act of deliverance of a person or institution or society from its bondage to evil, and its restoration to the wholeness intrinsic to its creation."[4] Exorcisms address the demonic powers—both spiritual and institutional—that hold individuals and communities captive. Such exorcisms were one of the central characteristics of Jesus' messianic mission, which he passed on to his followers. They were a central element of Jesus' apocalyptic struggle with the powers. As preachers, we are called, like Jesus' disciples, to continue this ministry. We are called to draw the demonic powers into the open—to name them and expose them, to silence their babble and refute their claims, and to cast them out with the word of the living God. We are called, in short, to perform homiletical exorcisms that set people free from the powers of death that imprison them.

To put this in other—possibly more palatable—language, preaching today needs to have a fundamentally *redemptive* purpose. Preachers should seek to speak a word that enables the people of God to step into the freedom from the powers of death given through Jesus' life, death, and resurrection. Here redemption takes on its original connotations of release from bondage, and the purpose of preaching becomes empowering the community of faith to step out of the open tomb and begin to live now in the way of the crucified and risen Jesus. Preaching, in other terms, comes to involve "raising the dead in mind and conscience" and empowering the church to live faithfully in the face of death.[5]

Within this overarching redemptive purpose, the focus of critique in preaching changes. Sermons will not be directed against persons, just as Jesus does not critique the possessed people, but rather challenges the demonic powers that hold them captive. As the writer of Ephesians puts it, "For our struggle is not against enemies of blood and flesh, but against the rulers, against the authorities, against the cosmic powers of this present darkness, against the spiritual forces of evil in the heavenly places" (Ephesians 6:12). Rather than making the people in the pews the enemy, the preacher focuses critique on the powers of death that hold people captive. The preacher does not stand against the congregation, but rather stands with them as one who also struggles with complicity in the face of the powers; all stand together in need of redemption through the Word. The preacher does not "beat up on people" or load them up with guilt, but rather seeks to set them free, possibly even tapping into their longing for release. Preaching thus moves beyond simplistically condemning or challenging individuals, and moves toward naming and confronting the powers that hold people captive. The "*tone*" of preaching consequently becomes more empathic and hopeful, rather than judgmental and angry.

Such homiletical exorcisms, however, do not just deal with the captivity of individuals. They also must address the captivity of the church itself. Indeed, Stringfellow emphasizes the political character of all the spiritual gifts, including exorcism. Exorcism is not simply an individual matter, but seeks to build up the church and enhance the church's servanthood on behalf of the world. It seeks to contribute to the restoration or renewal of human life in community so that the church may live faithfully in the face of the powers. Exorcism is fundamentally a communal act of resistance to the powers of death, and not just an individual one.[6]

The story of Jesus' exorcism in the Capernaum synagogue (Luke 4:31–37), for example, suggests that exorcisms deal not just with individuals, but also with religious institutions, including the church. That's the deeply disturbing part of the story. Jesus' encounter with the demon takes place in the *synagogue* on the *sabbath* (vv. 31, 33). He encounters the demonic at the very heart of the religious community's space and time. Indeed, Jesus' presence and speech in the synagogue may have so threatened the religious institution that he called out into the open a demon representing the religious "powers that be."[7]

We get a sense of the character of this demonic spirit in some of the words the demon speaks to Jesus. "Let us alone!" the demon cries out, fearing destruction. "What have you to do with us, Jesus of Nazareth? Have you come to destroy us?" (v. 34). The demon represents the *spirit of survival* at the heart of religious institutions, survival at all costs driven by the fear of death. Such survival is one of the priorities of the demonic powers and those held captive by them. And that spirit is alive right in the heart of the community of faith. And it is a deadly spirit that can hold the church captive. Indeed, at times it seems as if the church today has succumbed to that spirit. Survival at all costs seems to be the name of the game at a time when the church's power and prestige have been threatened by an increasingly secular culture. And when that happens, the church tends to go along with the powers of the world, to play it safe in order to offer an attractive face to potential members. In the process the sharp edges of the gospel are smoothed away, and the church often becomes little more than another appealing commodity for middle-class consumers. Ironically, in its quest for survival, the church succumbs to the powers of death, no longer providing the space and time within which people can be set free to live faithfully in the way of Jesus Christ. As a form of exorcism, preaching will need to name and "cast out" this spirit of survival from the heart of the church.

The next words of the demon in the synagogue follow predictably. "I know who you are, the Holy One of God" (v. 34). On the surface, this sounds like a profound confession. At the deepest level, however, these words represent an attempt to gain control of Jesus. In Jesus' day, if you could name someone, you would have that person in your power. Here in the midst of the community of faith, then, Jesus encounters the *spirit of control.* The demonic power seeks to control the Word, to make it safe, to take away its threatening, dangerous authority, so the institution can continue with business as usual. When the spirit of survival takes over, the spirit of control will not be far behind. When the purpose of the religious institution is to survive, it can't stand a word that is free and authoritative. It can't have a word that seeks to kill it and raise it from the dead. And as a consequence, it won't have a word and it won't be a community with the power to set people free. The demonic powers thus speak from the center of the church and present a striking institutional challenge to Jesus.

These powers also speak from the larger society. As a form of exorcism, preaching does not remain within the church, addressing the community of faith. Such preaching also confronts the social structures and institutions (including their spiritual force) that hold people captive to the powers of death. As a form of exorcism, preaching speaks a public word, seeking to address the "collective possession" that can hold societies captive.

In the gospel of Mark, as Ched Myers has so helpfully noted, this movement from the community of faith to the larger society becomes clear. Not long after his exorcism in the Capernaum synagogue (Mk. 1:21–28; par. Lk. 4:31–37), Jesus goes out into the world and encounters the powers of death in the form of the Gerasene demoniac (Mk. 5:1–20). Jesus confronts not the demonic power at the heart of the religious institution, but rather the spirit of Roman imperial power and oppression, which is embodied in a representative person. Jesus challenges the demonic power of *violent domination*, which characterizes empire and comes to characterize human relationships shaped by empire. Not surprisingly, this spirit lives in the tombs, for its ultimate power is death.

The Gerasene demoniac is possessed by "Legion," a technical term for a Roman military division. In constantly breaking his chains among the tombs, the demoniac acts out the community's repressed longing to be freed from their oppression and the death it brings to them. The demoniac represents in an external form the spirit of oppression and the repressed desire for freedom that possesses the entire community, and his presence among the people serves to maintain order in the community by keeping their violent resentment in check.

Jesus' exorcism of the Gerasene demoniac is thus a "public symbolic action" in which he confronts the powers of Roman imperialism that hold the community in their formidable grip.[8] Not surprisingly, when the people of the region hear that the demoniac is in his right mind, they are not pleased, but ask Jesus to leave. Their possession is so deep–their spirits are so captive–that they cannot even imagine liberation; they themselves have become more comfortable with their captivity to the Empire than with the possibility of freedom.

In the gospel of Mark, according to Myers, this exorcism, juxtaposed with Jesus' exorcism in the synagogue at Capernaum, represents Jesus' inaugural challenge to the powers. In Mark, Jesus prepares the "space" for his ministry with these two exorcisms, highlighting the character of his ministry as an engagement with the powers of death in the world. When Jesus appears in the synagogue—the institutional space of the religious authorities—a demon appears and seeks to control him by naming him. Similarly, when Jesus first appears on Gentile territory, a demon representing Roman imperial power appears, seeking to control him in the same way (Mark 5:7). The "powers that be," knowing the threat Jesus poses to the status quo, immediately seek to bring his work under their own authority. In both instances, Jesus exorcises these demonic powers as a symbolic political act.

> Put in military terminology, [these two exorcisms] signal the decisive breach in the defenses of the symbolic fortress of Roman Palestine. The political and ideological authority of both the scribal establishment and the Roman military garrison—the two central elements within the colonial condominium—have been repudiated. The narrative space has been cleared for the kingdom ministry to commence in full, both to Jew and gentile.[9]

Through his exorcisms, Jesus did not simply focus on individuals, but he addressed the institutional powers—both religious and political—that enslave people at both the material and spiritual levels.

In both the synagogue and Gerasea, moreover, Jesus exorcises these demonic powers through the *word.* Proclamation takes the form of exorcism. In the synagogue, in the face of the spirit of survival and control, Jesus responds, "Be silent, and come out of him!" (Lk. 4:35). And the spirit comes out. To the Roman imperial power of violent domination, Jesus proclaims, "Come out of the man, you unclean spirit!" (Mk. 5:8). And the spirit (after some negotiation in this case) leaves the man, enters a herd of swine, and runs off a cliff. In both instances, the word proclaimed by Jesus sets the captives free. And that is the good news for all who preach, for all who seek to lead the church, for all who ache for the freedom and faithfulness of the people of God. We may be captive to the powers of death, the society may be captive to the powers of death, and even the church may be captive to those powers. But the word of God is not.

"Be silent, and come out of him." says Jesus. "Come out of the man, you unclean spirit." With these words, proclamation becomes exorcism. The Word moves to set individuals and the society and the church free from the demonic powers that hold us captive. And through the freedom and authority of the Word, the demonic spirits come out. And people are set free. And society and church are set free. That is the good news that sustains us in our calling and gives us hope in our preaching. That is the good news that holds out the promise of freedom and life, even in the face of the demonic powers. And that is the good news that makes preaching exhilarating—and dangerous.

Preaching and Practices

Although homiletical exorcisms represent an important move in preaching that seeks to build up the community of faith for life in and for the world, this move alone is inadequate. As Jesus notes in Matthew 12:44–45, once a demon has been "cast out," seven more are waiting to take its place. The powers' assault on people is relentless. Consequently, once congregations have been set free from the powers of death, the old ways need to be replaced with new practices of discipleship that enable people to resist the powers and live faithfully in the world. Through such practices, freedom *from* the powers becomes freedom *for* faithful discipleship.

Just as Jesus understood the role of the word in exorcising the powers of death, so he understood the importance of practices in forming believers into a community of discipleship. At the conclusion of Matthew 12, following its thorough discussion of the demonic powers and exorcism, Jesus emphasizes the community of faith that "does the will" of God. Such a community, the text suggests, provides the concrete, embodied alternative to the ways of survival and control, domination and violence that often govern the world.

In the Sermon on the Mount (Mt. 5–7), Jesus similarly demonstrates the importance of communal practices for preaching. In the sermon Jesus seeks to constitute the new community of disciples who will embody his way of resistance to the powers of death. And the bulk of his sermon consists of a delineation of the practices that will shape this new community's life together in and for the world. In virtually every area of life, Jesus calls for practices that offer an alternative to the ways of the powers of death, domination, and violence. In this new community, the practice of reconciliation takes priority over vengeance (5:21–26); women are no longer treated as objects or property (5:27–32); love of enemies and nonviolent resistance replace violent domination of the "other" (5:38–48)[10]; religious practices do not become the source of superiority and competition (6:1–18); the desire for wealth is not the driving motivation of life (6:19–34). Socially, politically, religiously, and economically, Jesus provides new practices that shape the community of faith as an alternative to the domination and violence of the world.

As Jesus proclaims in his sermon, living as a redeemed people, who have been set free from captivity to the powers of death, involves engaging in practices that embody and nurture the community in the way of discipleship. Only through such practices will the community be able to resist the powers of death that continue to assault them on a daily basis. Consequently, like Jesus, contemporary preachers need to call churches to engage in new and faithful practices of resistance. And preachers need to issue this call in concrete, particular ways, offering specific practices that build up congregations as communities of resistance in and for the world.

Such a move to these practices has not been popular in contemporary homiletical theory. Recent approaches to preaching have advised preachers to leave sermons open so individuals can experience the gospel for themselves and draw their own conclusions for their lives. The indicative has reigned supreme, and "telling people what to do" has been virtually an anathema. Preachers are to engage in an open-ended conversation, rather than make any claims or demands upon the congregation.

There are, to be sure, good reasons for these current emphases. Moralistic preaching, which places human rules and works before the work of God in Jesus Christ, is counter to the gospel, transforming the gospel of God's gracious initiative into the burden of human efforts. Similarly, contemporary homileticians are rightly wary of preachers imposing their own agenda on a congregation—something that certainly happens all too frequently in the church. A preacher who seeks to dominate the congregation with his or her demands turns preaching itself into a practice shaped by control and domination. A healthy dose of suspicion at this point is essential to avoid moralistic, authoritarian, and often manipulative directives from the pulpit.

Such a healthy suspicion, however, should not deter preachers from exploring ways in which concrete practices may be nurtured from the pulpit. Jesus, after all, did not avoid this move to practices in his Sermon on the Mount. Likewise, Paul regularly makes a similar turn, as he moves from theological vision to ecclesial practices in the course of his letters. Such a homiletical move was critical for the gospels and for Paul, for they understood that the church's resistance to the powers is built up and sustained by concrete practices.

In addition, such practices should not simplistically be placed in opposition to God's redemptive Word, as is often suggested in positions emphasizing the dichotomy between grace and works. Practices can lead one into grace just as often as grace empowers practices. Engagement in the concrete practices of the Christian community may, in fact, become, not a means of works righteousness, but a means to coming into a fuller sense of God's redemption. In the gospels, for example, Jesus first invites the twelve to "follow me"; only on the journey of discipleship do the disciples come to sense the reality of their own sin and the power of God's grace. Similarly, it is only when the disciples on the road to Emmaus engage in the practice of hospitality to the stranger that they ultimately come to "see" the risen Lord and return to Jerusalem (the place of death) in the power of the new creation (Lk. 24:13–35). Dietrich Bonhoeffer was right: Grace is inseparable from the practices of discipleship; the relationship between the two is reciprocal, rather than one-directional.[11]

In seeking to nurture the congregation in new and renewed practices, then, preachers should not shy away from naming concrete practices that seem to emerge from the gospel.[12] At the same time, however, they should go about this calling in a particular way. Most generally, preachers will remember that preaching amidst the powers seeks to be a *redemptive* activity. In building up a community of resistance, the preacher seeks to set people free from captivity to the powers. In preaching about practices, preachers will keep this redemptive purpose in mind. Such preaching will not be based on guilt, which tends to cripple people rather than free them for action. Nor will such preaching seek to motivate people through fear. Fear of being punished if one does not engage in the correct practices turns the gospel into a burden.[13] Neither guilt nor fear serve the purposes of redemptive proclamation.

Such preaching also avoids moralizing, "in which one person seeks to prescribe behavior for another but from outside the horizon of that other person."[14] While the preacher may clearly name and clarify the importance of particular practices, these cannot be imposed upon people from the outside, but must grow from within the life of the community. Nurturing faithful practices through preaching is thus necessarily part of a larger process of discernment within a community of ethical discourse, in which believers struggle together "to embrace specific patterns of practice by which a gospel perspective can be lived out in its concrete circumstances."[15] Preachers may "sow seeds," but their growth depends on the work of the Spirit, the larger life and conversation of the community, and other ecclesial practices. Within this larger context, preaching should be understood as one particular practice–albeit an important one– within the community's entire life understood as a "school of practice."[16]

Within this context, however, preachers should not hesitate in sermons to name and nurture particular communal practices within the congregation. While preachers can do this in a variety of ways, I would like to suggest three possible approaches.

First of all, and most broadly, preachers can present these practices as a grateful response to God's acts of redemption. God takes the initiative to set people free from the powers of death in the world, and the church's practices represent the thankful response of God's people for all that God has done. Examples of this kind of turn to practices abound in Scripture. For example, in Romans 12:1 Paul writes: "I appeal to you, therefore, brothers and sisters, by the mercies of God, to present your bodies as a living sacrifice, holy and acceptable to God, which is your spiritual worship." Paul then proceeds in the remainder of the letter to delineate various practices that flesh out the community's response to God's mercies. Similarly, this move is typical in the Old Testament. The Ten Commandments themselves are presented in Exodus 20 as a response to God's redemptive activity on behalf of the people of Israel. The list of commandments opens with the reminder of God's work: "I am the Lord your God, who brought you out of the land of Egypt, out of the house of slavery…" (v.2). Only then is the community given the set of practices for living into the redemption that God has accomplished for them. Such a move to practices, based on the gracious initiative of God, will keep preachers from moralizing and from depending on guilt or fear as motivations for the community's practices of discipleship.

Second, within an apocalyptic framework, exorcisms can be understood as the inbreaking of the new creation, and practices may be presented as the means for participating in that new creation. Through Jesus' apocalyptic work, a "new space" of freedom and life has been opened up in the midst of the powers, and particular practices offer the means for living into that new reality. While recognizing the continuation of the "old age" and the suffering it brings, the preacher nevertheless invites the church to begin living now in the new creation in order to embody before the world a new possibility in the midst of the old.

The apostle Paul takes this approach in Galatians 3:28 when he announces the new space opened up by Jesus—in Christ there is no longer Jew or Greek, slave or free, male and female—and calls the community of baptized Christians to live into that new reality. As Nancy Duff writes,

> Paul is not...proposing an "interim ethic" showing us how to live in the Old Age before the New Age arrives. Although we must be alert to the dangers of enthusiasm, we nevertheless live *now* in that new space created by the powerful invasion of Christ. Living within that new space we can no longer tolerate the Old Age distinctions in the social and political order which oppress and destroy. We refuse to allow the political order which has foundations in the Old Age to operate under the slogan "business as usual," because we do not recognize its legitimacy in God's world. It is in that new space created in Christ that the church is called into being and action.[17]

After helping the congregation see and experience the new creation that has broken into the world, the preacher may then turn to particular practices as the means for living into this new reality. In this way, the turn to practices is not burdensome but redemptive— and possibly even exciting!

A third way of approaching practices redemptively is through praise—praise for those "saints" who have lived free from the powers of death and embodied excellence in a particular practice. Jesus takes this approach in Matthew 12:49–50 when he praises the community of believers who do God's will, calling such people his mother and brothers and sisters. Jesus holds up a specific community for others to emulate.

David DeSilva has highlighted this approach in the book of Hebrews. By providing a host of exemplars of the virtues of trust and firmness in 10:32–12:3, the author of Hebrews "sets out to praise those who have embodied the course he is advising. The effect of this encomium should be the arousal of the emotion of emulation: the hearers are encouraged and even made ambitious to embody the same virtue as these figures who have attained a praiseworthy resemblance."[18] Just as any practice has a history of practitioners who have achieved excellence in the practice and set new standards for it, so the practices of Christian discipleship have such "virtuoso performers," whom we call saints. Recognizing the importance of such practitioners, the preacher of Hebrews holds before the congregation the lives and practices of these saints in order to inspire believers to similar faithfulness.[19]

Like the preacher of Hebrews, contemporary preachers may tell the stories of virtuoso practitioners from the history of the Christian tradition. In addition, preachers may wish to highlight contemporary saints, particularly those "everyday" saints within the congregation who embody particular practices in exemplary ways. Finally, preachers may wish to tell the stories of particular Christian *communities*, past or present, whose life together embodies the excellence of particular practices. By sharing these lives and stories, the preacher doesn't seek to make people feel guilty, but to hold forth the possibility of life set free from the powers of death. Such stories, as DeSilva argues, do not need to become a burden, but can rather be an inspiration grounded in the gracious redemption of God.

In various ways, then, preachers may move through homiletical exorcisms and help build up Christian communities in the practices that enable them to live in resistance to the powers and embody an alternative to the ways of domination, violence, and death. Such preaching does not come easily; it is a fragile and risky undertaking, which at times can seem both foolish and audacious. And, as Luther reminded us, it calls preachers to a "most dangerous kind of life," which requires imagination and courage and, most of all, a deep hope in the living word of God. Nevertheless, such foolish and risky preaching, which dares to confront the powers and build up the church, continues to be essential for the faithfulness of God's people and the life of God's world.

Seeing Jesus

Preaching as Incarnational Act

JANA CHILDERS

What is preaching meant to do? The question is a timely one. We are hardly living in homiletics' Golden Age, after all. Time-honored forms of preaching are discarded every week, the new and novel grabbed up. What principles should guide such divesting and reinvesting? A clear sense of what we are trying to achieve would, at the very least, be helpful. Yet, many preachers seem reticent about declaring themselves on the subject.

Even the field of Homiletics itself has been restrained. Lucy Rose speaks for many young (and some not-so-young) scholars in the discipline when she tells of being asked, some years after she began teaching Homiletics at Columbia Theological Seminary, to give her definition of the purpose of preaching. "I realized I didn't have one," she said. To her credit, she promptly set about a study of the question. It was this work which led ultimately to her seminal book *Sharing the Word: Preaching in the Roundtable Church.*

Rose discovered that though there are now and have always been different ways to define preaching's purpose, most models may be organized into three categories: in "traditional"[1] preaching, the aim is clearly persuasion, or as Rose described it in an early essay, "to win consent from the congregation to a truth claim"[2]; in "kerygmatic"[3] preaching the purpose is "to communicate the unchanging heart of the gospel"[4]; in "transformational" preaching "whatever else a sermon does, its primary purpose is to facilitate an experience, an event, a meeting, or a happening for the worshipers."[5]

Rose's research led her to propose another category. She granted that "sometimes preaching accomplishes one of the three aims purported by the dominant theories. But, in addition, preaching's goal at times is to gather the community of faith around the Word."[6] It is this understanding of preaching that led Rose to formulate the "conversational" model of preaching, a model that seeks to de-center the preacher's authority and share the responsibility and privilege of interpreting scripture more widely. Stated more fully, conversational preaching's aim is "week after week to gather the community of faith around the Word in order to foster and refocus its central conversations."[7]

In the five years since Rose proposed what may be the first new understanding of preaching's purpose in seventy-five years, the conversation about conversation has flourished. Rose's premature death (at the age of fifty, from breast cancer) leaves the table feeling emptier, but the lively discussion continues, spurred for many by the freshness of her ideas. At the very least, Rose's proposal leaves us wondering, "Are there still newer models of preaching that preachers and homileticians should be exploring?"; "Does the purpose of preaching change over time, or just the trappings?"; "Is it possible to articulate an understanding of preaching's purpose that encompasses all preaching?" In other words, Rose stirred an important pot and left us each asking our own version of The Question: "What, exactly, do we think we are doing?" In an age like ours, it's an important question to ask.

Seeing Jesus

"Sir, we [would] see Jesus." The reference is to a passage in the gospel of John. "Some Greeks" apply to Philip for admittance to Jesus' presence (Jn. 12:20–21). Probably they are there because they want to meet the miracle worker who raised Lazarus from the dead—or maybe they just want a close-up view of Jerusalem's newest hero. Perhaps, though, they have real questions they are anxious to put to Jesus. Perhaps, we might fantasize, they are orators drawn by the power of his words and eager to know the secret of that power. We don't know, of course. We don't know because John doesn't editorialize; he simply reports the sequence of events. He tells us that Philip takes the Greeks' request to Andrew, and the two disciples approach Jesus together. Jesus answers them with a long discourse about his own death and the cost of following him. We never find out what happened to the Greeks.

Their words, however, are immortalized on certain small plaques placed in many modern pulpits. Tacked along the bottom edge of the lectern, they are designed to catch the preacher's eye as the preacher enters the pulpit. "Sir, we would see Jesus." Some elder thought it would be a good idea to remind the preacher, perhaps. Or maybe some retiring pastor provided it as advice to a successor. If there is any one sentiment that represents the spirit of the previous generation of preachers, it is the one captured on these little brass plates.

Among the preachers of this generation, reaction to those pious reminders varies widely. Those of us who are not "sirs" have been known to snicker at the sight. Others, coming across one for the first time, report a shiver. Those who have been around many homiletical barns sometimes admit to a feeling of discouragement.

Is this what preaching is meant to do? To help people "see Jesus"? Is this preaching's purpose, its *raison d'être*? How can preaching be said to cause, facilitate, or even approximate such a thing? These days, holding the attention of the listeners is as much as many preachers can manage. Is it possible for a twenty-first century preacher to do more than that? What would it mean to see Jesus, anyway? Even if our sermons could manage to "hold up a picture" of Jesus, what makes us think anyone would care about it, much less be drawn to and changed by it?

Our questions about the nature and purpose of preaching do not have easy answers.

Small plates engraved with a few words lifted out of an ambiguous narrative are of limited use to those of us who fret over the current state of preaching. Who could blame us if we felt a little like those curious Greeks who politely asked for help, and ended up standing on one foot and then the other? We are entitled, are we not, to feel a little dyspeptic as, growing frustrated, we glance over at Philip's and Andrew's hunched backs?

However impatient we are with the questions contemporary preaching raises in us, we might think twice before taking the screwdrivers to all those brass plates. Before we vandalize the spiritual wisdom of the ancestors, we might hold the words up to twenty-first century light and ask if "seeing Jesus" has any meaning for us.

Preaching Christ

Lacking a Philip to intercede on our behalf, many of us take our question about preaching's nature and purpose to the Bible, only to find that Scripture has its own ways of talking about preaching. The Bible uses several syntactical settings of the word. Matthew favors the plain-Jane subject and predicate: "Jesus began to preach" (Mt. 4:17, RSV) or "they preach" (23:3). Luke includes kingdom language: Jesus sends the disciples out to "preach the kingdom of God" (9:2, RSV). Mark and Paul both seem to lean toward "preach the gospel" (Mk. 16:15; 1 Cor. 1:17, RSV). Though the last turns out to be the most favored combination, New Testament language mandates no one usage. No single syntactical setting for the word *preach* is even heavily favored. Instead, scripture presents us with a pliable word that may mean slightly different things in different contexts.

Much of the New Testament's view of preaching, however, is caught up in and held together by one particular phrase: "We preach Christ." The peculiar quality of it alone draws our attention. Richard Lischer has demonstrated "how saturated with Christ that early proclamation was," by listing some of the objects of the New Testament verbs for *preach.* He includes: "Jesus, Lord Jesus, Christ, Jesus Christ as Lord, Christ crucified, Christ as raised from the dead, Jesus and the resurrection, good news about the Kingdom, Jesus as the Son of God, the gospel of God, Word of the Lord, the forgiveness of sins, and Christ in you—the hope of glory."[8]

Among them all, "We preach Christ" is not only the most peculiar but perhaps the most evocative. For some longtime Christians, the mere mention of the phrase stirs memories of old-fashioned church signs, "We Preach Christ Crucified, Risen and Coming Again." There used to be many of those signs. There used to be many church lawns displaying the sentiment. And there used to be many kids thinking, "What does that mean?" Does it mean, as some surely assume, that we preach about Christ—about the wounded side, the dewy garden grass, the trumpet sound? Does it mean that we preach in or through Christ—with a spiritual power unique to him, but shared somehow with us? Does it mean that we preach under his banner or his authority? That our words are subject finally to some standard of his? How is it that a person can be preached?

No one would be under any obligation, of course, to pursue such questions or even to give all those old-fashioned signs a second thought, if it weren't for the fact that the slogan is so strategically important in New Testament theology: "We preach Christ." They are the words of no one less than the apostle Paul. "For since, in the wisdom of God, the world did not know God through wisdom, it pleased God through the folly of what we preach to save those who believe. For Jews demand signs and Greeks seek wisdom, but we preach Christ crucified" (1 Cor. 1:21–23, RSV). As some old-fashioned congregations have always known, there is more than a soupçon of power and mystery associated with the particular phrase, "We preach Christ." What does it mean?

I think it means that preaching is an incarnational act, paralleling in pattern and process the form of God's self-revelation. If this is true, or at least represents one of the layers of that powerful, enigmatic phrase, it suggests something about both the nature and the purpose of preaching. First, we will consider briefly how incarnational preaching might be defined, and then return to the question of what it is meant to do.

Incarnational Preaching: Christ as Pattern and Process

The parallel between the form of the Incarnation and the form of the preacher's work is striking.[9] For preachers, as for other artists, the creative act is one of collaboration that is quite similar in pattern to the Incarnation. Incarnation may be said to happen when two entities come together and produce a third entity that embodies them both, and in which the integrity of each is still maintained.[10] In the case of Christ, the first two entities were, of course, the two natures, divine and human. The product of their union was Jesus Christ himself. In the case of preaching, the first two entities may be understood as preacher and text, or as preacher and Holy Spirit, or as preacher and Holy Spirit working through the text and context...and the third entity the sermon.

The similarity between the structure of human creative process and the divine creative process involved in the Incarnation of Jesus Christ is not only striking but, once one gets used to the definition of incarnation offered above, seems obvious. What is not so self-evident is that what is incarnated in each case is not the material elements we are used to thinking of, or the elements of "substance" spoken of by the ancient church, or even elements of "spirit" more generically defined. What is incarnated in the Incarnation and in every act of homiletical creativity is action. As Charles Bartow has so helpfully said, "the Word of God is not *verbum* but *sermo*, not *ratio* but *oratio*. It is lively, face to face aural-oral discourse and suasory action...It is *actio divina*, God's self-performance..."[11] In the incarnational view then, preaching Christ means participating in the ongoing action of God, of coming together with and being caught up in the unfolding of God's business at work in the world. In incarnational preaching, preaching Christ means more than speaking.

Similarly, preaching Christ means more than speaking about Jesus Christ. Christ is more than the content of our preaching. Describing Jesus' personality, explaining Christological doctrine, drawing practical tips for moral living from Jesus' teaching, or rehashing the search for the historical Jesus will not keep anybody awake very long. As Rosenstock-Huessy says, "When we speak about something, we do less than we are expected to do. When we chat about God and the world, our mind is on vacation. And this chatter, gossip, talk is the shell or the chaff of the real and full power of speech when things speak through us."[12] It is the notion of *throughness* that is important. In this notion we begin to see the parallels between preaching's process and that of the Incarnation. In the Incarnation, the quintessential example of what Rosenstock-Huessy calls "real and full speech," the word of God is mediated *through* Christ. Similarly, God spoke *through* prophets and speaks *through* preachers. As the writer of Hebrews says, "In many and various ways God spoke of old to our fathers by the prophets; but in these last days, [God] has spoken to us by a Son" (Heb. 1:1–2, RSV).

It is a simple concept with commonsense appeal. What could be more obvious than to say that whatever it means to "preach Christ," it at least means that the preacher will allow the Word or the Spirit or *Something* to work *through* him or her? The kind of emphasis on *throughness* that we are talking about, however, is not as popular as one might think. In an interview with *The New York Times,* the founding pastor of a well-known megachurch explained the model that informs his ministry. He expressed a particular concern for the loss of the Baby Boom generation from the ranks of church membership:

> [H]e said that he had discerned a "tearing of the fabric" in the 1960's and 1970's, as droves of young people quit church. Now middle-aged with children of their own, they can be coaxed back, he said, if a minister shows them Scripture's relevance to their lives. That means strategizing to discover the right contemporary wrapper (music, for one) in which to present a timeless Gospel message.[13]

Many preachers agree. A better "wrapper" or a smarter marketing strategy is what many are looking for and, of course, they have a point. Presentation is almost everything. There is a great deal to be said for wrappers.

Next to the contemporary emphasis on the outer aspects of preaching—on "wrapping" or "presentation" or "dressing up" or "curb appeal"—I would like to set an alternative model. The understanding of preaching that emphasizes throughness represents a model that is interested in the inner. It is a model that expects preachers to "outer what they inner." Preachers who understand their craft this way prioritize a skill called "internalization," a discipline that undergirds preachers' attempts to embody the words they speak. Words are not regarded as tools, but as agents of self-disclosure and immediacy. Such preachers believe there should be a match between the words of their mouths and the meditations of their hearts. Words and inner experience are congruent, all the time—or as much as is humanly possible. It is this sincere, internalized, natural-sounding speech that provides a faithful vehicle for preaching Christ.

This understanding of what Rosenstock-Huessy called "real" or "full power" speech is anything but new. It puts to use the ancient insights of actors and prophets—as well as Jesus' own ministry. It combines the age-old artists' disciplines of concentration, imagination, and observation. It is perhaps best expressed, and certainly most famously represented, in the homiletical theory of a nineteenth-century preacher. But it seems an especially timely word and an appropriate model of preaching for those who must try to get a hearing from the jaded listeners of the twenty-first century.

It was Phillips Brooks, of course, who said it first, best, and one hundred twenty years ago: "Truth through personality." His lectures at Yale called upon preachers to attend to their innards—to let the truth of God *invade* them. "The truth must really come *through* a person, not merely over his lips, not merely into his understanding and out of his pen. It must come through his character—his affections—his whole intellectual and moral being."[14] There are only two kinds of preachers, Brooks believed. "The gospel has come over one of them and reaches us tinged and flavored with his superficial characteristics, belittled by his littleness. The gospel comes through the other and we receive it impressed and winged with all the earnestness and strength that there is in him."[15]

The aspect of Brooks's throughness that is most neglected in contemporary preaching is also the one that I believe is most potentially helpful to twenty-first-century preachers. It has to do with the performance phase of the throughness, the end phase, the phase that is about the preacher "being present in the words" while standing in the pulpit or speaking them. In this brief exploration of throughness, I have focused on this aspect not because it is in itself the most important of all the pieces of preaching's process (surely the development of a preacher's character, spiritual formation, ethical reflection, and theological commitments deserve all the time they can get!), but because it is the most neglected, because it has the potential to address this generation's famous criticism of preachers (their apparent lack of sincerity), and because it suggests an approach that is a better fit for the media-drunk listener.

In summary, an incarnational understanding of preaching suggests that a primary purpose of preaching is *continuity*. Why preach? Because, the incarnational preacher will reply, the gospel wants *continuing*. Not only does it want continuing, it wants continuing in lived experience—in the acts of real people, preachers and listeners. Alla Bozarth-Campbell describes it this way, "In making the word to become flesh, the interpreter makes herself or himself into the word, takes the word as poem into her or his body, continues the creation process begun by the past."[16] Bozarth is speaking, from a literary point of view or an oral interpretation theory point of view, about allowing the word of the text to achieve "bodily entelechy" in the preacher, but the same may be said to be the goal of preaching in a more general sense. The listeners are meant to embody the Word, too—right down the aisles and out into the world. It is in this sense, then, that the purpose of preaching is a certain kind of action. One might say the purpose of preaching is to make something happen. The kind of thing that "something" turns out to be is not unimportant. But it is not nearly as important as making this distinction: Preaching's purpose is not defined in terms of ideas but of action.

Preaching is not static. It is not a thing. It is an act whose purpose it is to kick off the chain of cause and effect, to tip the end domino, to set motion in motion. Of all the kinds of movement preaching is interested in (and there are many—integrating personality and spirituality, inspiring love, comforting, producing belief, reinforcing faith, maintaining communion, stiffening sinews, conforming to the image of Christ, to name just a few personal favorites), one is chief above and precedes all others; one is the first step that leads to the others.

Openness

P. T. Forsyth puts it well, "God is not really opened to me till He opens me to Him. All this is possible if [preaching] be much more than declaration. It must be an act. Christ spoke far less of love than he practiced it. He did not publish a new idea of the Father–rather He was the first true Son."[17]

Openness is the kind of movement preaching is interested in before it is interested in any other. In some theological traditions, openness is regarded as the one thing human beings have to offer God; in others, God supplies even this. But whether a preacher is addressing Wesleyans or Calvinists, the preaching task is the same. To preach Jesus Christ is to allow God's Word to work through one's own personality and expressiveness in such a way that both preacher and congregation are opened.

We started with the question about what preaching "is meant to do." The word choice turns out to be significant. Perhaps when we put the matter more academically–"How does one define the purpose of preaching?"–we are more easily tempted toward abstraction. But the question, as we have posed it, contains something of its own answer. Preaching is, indeed, meant to do something. It is meant to make something happen. It is meant to open us or, at the very least, our eyes.

"Sir, we would see Jesus." When Philip and Andrew told Jesus what the Greeks had asked, Jesus replied, "The hour has come for [me] to be glorified (Jn. 12:23)." May it be so.

4

The Action Potential of Preaching

TERESA L. FRY BROWN

A lifetime ago I taught neurology, physiology, anatomy, and endocrinology classes to students in the Speech Pathology and Audiology program at a university in central Missouri. In conjunction with physicians' or educators' diagnosis of a speech-language disorder, speech-language pathologists evaluate language abilities of children and adults prior to programming communication skills or modifying behavior. Knowledge of organic, mechanical, and learned causative agents is essential to the effective treatment of individual speech and language problems. One of the principles of neuroscience that I remember is *action potential*. This is the momentary change in a nerve or muscle cell when the inner negative charge is impacted by an outer positive change. This depolarization is a rapid change in the permeability of the cell membrane.[1] The cell is stimulated by the transmission of a nerve impulse.[2] The action potential is the overall change in the nature of the cell. The entire process takes one-thousandth of a second. After a momentary rest (refractory period), the cycle begins again. This repetition results in neural impulses.[3] When a neuron is not sending a signal, it is in *resting potential.*

As I thought about the purpose of preaching, I began to draw parallels between these neurological states and the power and paucity of preaching the word of God. The communication of the word of

49

God is similar to that explosion of electrical activity across membrane of the nerve cell. The speaker shares information about God with a listener who may be experiencing questions, doubts, thoughts that are antithetical to God's plan and promise of life. The impulse of the word of God permeates the personal and communal walls or barriers by stimulating a change in one's negative charge—lack of faith, doubting faith, or need to reinforce personal belief—by introducing a positive charge—faith, acceptance, or belief. The result is a homiletical action potential. Unlike the neuron, which will return to the previous state and begin the process all over again, the word of God has potential for sustained energy. The action potential of the preached Word is reinforced through constant reiteration of the biblical stories, personal testimonies, and contemporary witness of the benefits of faith.

Homiletical resting potential takes place when personal and communal resistance to change disrupts the preaching moment. The purpose of preaching is dynamic (action potential), not stagnant (resting potential). The intent of preaching is to communicate means to faith development. It is concerned with the individual, communal, and global identity and vision. Preaching impacts the psychological and social healing, and reconciliation. Myth reinforcement and belief maintenance are critical factors in design of preaching. The purpose of preaching is to present the acknowledged word of God, regardless of translation, verbally and nonverbally with such presence, power, passion, and purpose that the listener or observer senses the impulse of change or conversion in his or her own life. Through sacred conversation channeled from God through the preacher with the people, transformation is effected.

The central focus of preaching is seeking to mine the mysteries of God—the who, what, when, where, how, and why of God—in relationship to God's creation. The inner being is bombarded with negative information; and through action potential, the positive message of God's promise for eternal life is shared, discussed, contemplated, and understood. The purpose of preaching is the proposition of the potentiality and actualization of healing the inner hurts and pains, deliverance from trial and tribulations, receipt of joys and blessings, and transformation from negative to positive life choices for the believer, nonbeliever, pretender, churched, unchurched, and dechurched. Preaching advocates a preferential option for opportunities to begin life anew. Preaching urges restoration of broken relationships, broken promises, broken people, broken dreams, broken communities, and broken beliefs. I believe that the core message of Christian preaching is entailed in Luke 4:18.

> "God's Spirit is on me;/he's chosen me to preach the Message of good news to the poor,/Sent me to announce pardon to prisoners and recovery of sight to the blind,/ To set the burdened and battered free, to announce, 'This is God's year to act!'"(Lk. 9:18, The Message)

The healing, saving, preaching, and teaching Jesus Christ of the New Testament sets the criterion for preaching about the critical concerns of the lives and lifestyles of all persons. The purpose of preaching is sharing good news through imparting the reception of social, physical, psychological, spiritual, and emotional freedom. It provides for spiritual vision and new ways of viewing life. Preaching projects the realization of God's presence in our lives. Preachers proclaim the possibility of change through assisting the listener in identification, examination, and resolution of alienation, conflict, and oppression located within the biblical text and society.

All persons have authority to proclaim, to tell others about the prophecy, birth, life, ministry, death, resurrection, and second coming (*parousia*) of Christ. The *kairos* or *fullness of time* is God's appointed time, place, and person(s) that occur to actualize God's promise. God is the eternal in the midst of time. Christian preaching is sustained through the proclamation of the biblical text and the transformative images and messages of Jesus. There is a confidence that the biblical text holds the key to how we are to live. It is not God's intention for persons to suffer continually. Sin is said to be the root cause for humanity's barriers, oppression of others, and lack of love for one another. Through telling and retelling stories of salvific incidents of God's self-revelation, preachers tell about action and promises in human history; and preaching's purpose is accomplished. Preaching reinforces the "wasness" (history) of God, who God is in the life of the faithful. Preaching establishes the "isness" (presence) in the here and now and then and there. Preaching delineates the "oughtness" (expectations) of God for human intrapersonal and interpersonal behavior and responsibility. Preaching interprets the "aboutness" (future actions) of God in the lives of the faithful and the unfaithful. The sustaining action potential of the word of God is entrusted to men and women who boldly state their interpretation of God's call on our lives. The purpose of preaching is to visualize pregnant possibilities of transformation of individuals, communities, nations, and the world from depressed, debilitated, disenfranchised, disrespected, disinterested, destructive, and depreciated entities into constructive, conscientious, creative, cooperative, connected, confident, and Christlike beings.

The responsibility of preachers is to explicate themselves, the biblical text, the congregation, and the contemporary situation in order to speak the truth in love. Preachers do not have all the answers and need to work through many of the same issues operating in the lives of the listeners. Preachers do not spoon-feed the faith but speak words of empowerment so that the thirsty can find their own water. The preacher provides templates of how to live in the present based on biblical imperatives. There is no monolithic interpretation of the biblical text. Commentaries aside, a textual hermeneutic is the extemporaneous understanding that evolves after a thorough reading and exegesis of a passage.

The preacher is the oral interpreter of the written text in the life of a particular context at a particular time, for a particular purpose. The preacher aids in reconstructing visions of shalom as the storm rages around the listener. The sermon provides hope-filled reconstruction of community with God at the center and fully in control. The preacher lets the listeners know that regardless of the concrete nature of life, God is at work. Prayers have been and are being answered. Liberation is not yet, but soon. Through compassion, love, genuine concern, and investment in the text, the preacher builds a level of trust with the congregation.

The preaching moment is either a life-giving or death-dealing communicative encounter where the trust of persons in "all good things of God" hangs in the balance. My personal assessment of the state of preaching begins with the resting potential of preaching, elements that may interfere with communication of the word of God. I avoid use of the terms "good" or "great" or "outstanding" as descriptors of preachers or sermons. I believe that the terms are overused. Every preacher has days when all homiletical elements are aligned, and others where nothing seems to work. There are negative forces that directly influence the consistent, positive, or substantive nature of preaching.

My personal experiences of listening to a number of sermons in preaching classes, various television ministries, commercial videotape sermons, preaching conferences, denominational worship services, Internet worship services, and discussions with clergy and laity on what is considered "good" preaching or a "great sermon" yields as many different standards as there are people. The assessment of the soundness of preaching is determined by the both the speaker and listener's experience, memory, tastes, distractions, idiosyncrasies, history, learning style, attention span, biblical literacy, and faith development.

The controlling image of the preacher has generally been of a male; tall, attractive, and humorous, with a deep voice, black clothing, booming projection, and commanding presence. The image of electronic preacher appears to be the standard in this century. The media preacher sports cassocks replete with collars, crosses, and chevrons. Tailored suits, hand microphone, head sets, computers, projection screens, television cameras, background music, Plexiglas podiums, notebooks, large Bibles, a cadre of ministers in support, large amphitheaters, mass choirs, handkerchiefs, and props could put Elmer Gantry to shame. There are also stereotypes of the preacher, usually based in inexplicable tradition. All preachers are men of God. Women of God are speakers who weep. Baptists, Pentecostals, and Charismatics preach while Presbyterians, Methodists, and Roman Catholics teach. African Americans' sound and movement are worthy of imitation, while others are tepid storytellers who are tolerated. Likewise, there is a move to emulate the voice, movement, style, theology, language, delivery, dress, and mannerisms of "big preachers" in apparent spiritual cloning or "being like Mike (and sometimes Michelle)" rather than developing individual homiletical portfolios. Authority for preaching emanates from God's call on one's life, not from some nebulous social construct.

Preaching lacks action potential when the gospel message is diluted to appease the listeners or play to the crowd for popularity rather than challenge and conversion. Sermons packaged in clichés, T-shirt slogans, or catch phrases that transcend denominations, gender, or geography may be fun and result in tape sales but may not have a lasting effect in the day-to-day lives of the people. The ability to reach the hearts and minds of the listeners with carefully chosen words, images, movements, and voice is often supplanted by love affairs with microphones and technical trappings. The overused hook of what musicologist James Abbington calls *charismania*[4] permeates many sermons. Commands of "Turn to your neighbor," "Give someone a high five," "Stand up," "Sit down," "Say Amen," "Somebody ought to say something," "You don't understand me," and, "I wish someone would help me up in here," punctuate sermons and serve as transition points or Pavlovian behavior modification bells for church calisthenics. Described by some as contemporary call and response, the physicality of the preacher and listener at times surpasses the content of the sermon.

Preaching at times seems to be a competition based on the number of call-in supporters, money raised, size of church, size of building, number of "armor bearers" and ministers on staff or conference invitations. Biblical stories and themes are overshadowed by emphasis on personal piety–promoted as prosperity; me-mine; me first; name it, claim it theology–and begging God for blessings. Some sermons are replete with popular or consumerist psychology based on an index of human needs rather than human responsibility. Formulaic, well-worn texts are recycled due to appeal or responsiveness of the listeners as if there were no other words in the Bible. Preaching has become the spotlight event in trendy worship rather than an integral part of the total worship experience. Memorization of Internet stories, latest movie lines, or popular songs paired with the three stories and a joke leave little room for the biblical text. Insertion of stories, images, and illustrations with little or no consideration of their appropriateness, connection to the biblical text, or experience of the listeners creates a moment of denied potential. The practice of prooftexting and referencing numerous texts with little or no exegesis, in the name of a "teaching" sermon, masks the power of the texts and their effectiveness in faith development. A number of sermons are disorganized, lacking focus or purpose, and seemingly have no ownership by the preacher. Finally, the resting potential of contemporary preaching is exemplified in linguistically biased, oppressive proclamation entrenched in diatribes on one's ethnicity, age, race, gender, sexuality, denomination, residence, economic status, physical ability, education, or health status.

The action-potential (transformative) homiletic begins with an understanding of the preacher's faith and of why he or she is preaching in the first place. It is an examination of the difference between public speaking and sacred speech. The awesomeness of the task of speaking God's Word is a point I must say that is missed by a number of "preachers." Preaching is not a game or something one does because she has nothing else to do, but rather a privileged faith activity. It is not something one does because he thinks he will gain popularity, but a responsibility that may alienate some people, yet lead others to life-changing decisions.

I begin the Introduction to Preaching classes with a discussion of "What is preaching?" and "Why me?" Prior to launching into speaking the word of God, one must have an idea of what one is doing. The preaching moment is not a place for cheap grace or quick fix but for patient endurance, anticipation, and confidence that the end of the matter is at hand not yet but soon. The sermon is more than a theoretical exercise in biblical scholarship. It is also a practical, day-in, day-out application of faith to a particular situation.[5] Preaching is ministry that focuses on the head, heart, and soul of the individual. Following exegesis of the congregation, the preacher launches into textual exegesis. The two work together in effective preaching. Many sermons miss their mark when there is no connection with the listeners. One should be pastoral before one becomes the prophet in the pulpit.

Pastoral preachers have some idea that they preach to living, breathing, hurting, happy, achieving, inquisitive, intelligent, and seeking individuals. Pastoral preachers are invested in pointing the way to salvation for all persons, not just the big tithers. Pastoral preachers understand that what they do not say is just as important as what is said. The presence of the preacher in the life events of the parishioners eases the acceptance of a compelling Word as well as the humor life affords. The pastoral preacher sees potential in everyone and hopes in the movement of God in the lives of believers and nonbelievers.

The prophetic preacher challenges the listener and self to change. The prophetic preacher is more than smoke and mirrors, hellfire and brimstone, or sound and fury, but is also passionate and authentic. He or she is more interested in spreading God's truth than in a personal title. The prophetic preacher is much more than loud voices, pounding fists, dramatic pauses, profuse sweating, flushed cheeks, and agile gesticulations. The prophetic preacher stands under God's Word and transmits God's message of transformation and living standards. Through moral discourse, the prophetic preacher creatively tells about our lives as God's children. Moral discourse establishes or describes the particular and universal value system or a particular context. The prophetic preacher, for example, may weave an ethic of care and concern, compassion, mutuality, cooperation, reverence, respect, responsibility, reconciliation, restraint, solidarity, community, gender or ethnic or racial pride, justice, love, liberation, hospitality, cooperation, or commitment to the survival of all persons into the body of the sermon.[6]

I contend that preaching is like teaching people to talk. Through repetitious instruction and reinforcement, the speaker pronounces a sound or word correctly, ceases stuttering, or remembers a concept. The point of change is not known, but the result is overwhelming. There is a sense of accomplishment on the part of the teacher and the learner. In preaching one does not know when the listener "gets it," but the modification in language and praxis of faith is just as powerful.

Teaching an introductory preaching class or a seminar on preaching is reminiscent of my speech pathology days. Small-step programming hopefully results in learned behavior that furthers the communicative cycle so that others receive information with minimal interference. I share several fundamental guidelines with new preachers. Preachers should spend time investigating what they believe, learning what the listeners believe, and receiving what God's Word says about those beliefs. A foundational theological (Who is God?) and Christological (Jesus Christ's life, ministry, teachings, crucifixion, resurrection, and second coming) discussion assists the members of the class or group in identifying others' belief systems, so there are fewer surprises during actual preaching events.

I ask the students to exegete themselves prior to entering into conversation with the biblical text. Questions include: What do I believe? Who is God in my life? What is my image of God? How do I speak about God? Who is God in my denomination? Who is Christ? Is Jesus a co-sufferer, co-laborer, and savior? How do I talk about the Holy Spirit? What is forgiveness? How are God's promises actualized? What are my hopes? Though not all persons are able to articulate or begin to understand their answers, they ask more questions in an attempt to preach about the subjects.

Understanding social location, worldview, and culture of the preacher and the congregation provides filters for word choice, phraseology, and delivery forms. Basic principles of rhetoric as well as kerygma are presented. Sorting out who or what validates them as preachers, by whose or what authority, precedes the initiation of a preaching ministry. The preaching moment is God centered, not preacher centered. It is really not about us. We serve merely as conduits for transmission of God's Word.

The sermon should be true to the biblical text. Students are encouraged to review at least five to seven different translations of the selected text, and compare and contrast the information. The text is the focus of sacred speech. We frame or weave that text with illustrations, images, phrases, songs, poems, or stories that illuminate rather than overshadow the word of God. Preaching is a dialogue rather than monologue or soliloquy. Preachers are charged to look, listen, and speak at the same time. It is in the preaching moment that lives are changed, including that of the preacher.

We do not preach in isolation; it is a communal event. We are neither the first nor the last to explore and preach a particular text. Textual selection depends on the denomination, use of lectionary, belief in the unction of the Holy Spirit, the church year, the occasion, and the preacher's personal preference. There are those who believe that they possess the definitive example of what a text means or how it should be preached. Their limited vision leads to egomaniacal preaching. They set themselves up as the standard without envisioning the individuality of the gifts and talents of preachers. Establishing continuity between the biblical text and the contemporary world is critical to listener understanding. When teaching a child a new sound or word, the teacher finds it essential to use an associated object or picture. In preaching, the mystery of the biblical text is easier to grasp when it is associated with the listener's life. Relevant, applicable sermons are more likely to lead to spiritual transformation.

There are endless sermonic forms or styles. I encourage preachers to explore several until they find the ones that fit them.

As a communication specialist, I find that the orality and aurality of the sermon form a significant focus of my teaching about sermon delivery. Persons preach the first day in class as a means of both breaking the ice and allowing me to hear their voices. They preach thereafter as the opportunity presents itself. Practice may not make preaching perfect, but it is certainly helpful in developing the skill. The length of the sermon runs from one to twenty minutes with videotape analysis and peer critiques. Students' articulation, dialect, volume, tone, fluency, breath control, presence, carriage, posture, rate, projection, and inflection are reviewed following lectures on speech and hearing production. Referrals to therapists or doctors are made when necessary.

The exchange of information between preacher and people is based on the experiences they share. Call and response is verbal or nonverbal feedback between the preacher and the people. Occasionally the preacher uses repetition—restatement of sound, word, and phrase for emphasis. Verbal and nonverbal signs, signals, and symbols represent the climate of beliefs, attitudes, values, common sense, and common talk in both the preacher and listener. The body language of the preacher, use of hands, movement in the pulpit space or into the congregation seating area, stance behind the podium, use of the microphone, handling of distractions, and energy or engagement with the listeners is also reviewed.

The preacher's facial expression holds a wealth of information. The emotion of the preacher is curiously also part of the oral presentation of the sermon. My contention is that although one is called to lead or minister with the people, one is also called as a passionate, compassionate human with emotions that need to be expressed. The skill is that one does not "bleed all over the congregation," beat up the congregation, expose too much of the self, or ignore the emotional temperature of the listener. Frowning while talking about the joy of the Lord creates confusion in the minds of the observer. Laughter during a statement about a tragic situation signifies fear, nervousness, or lack of emotional sensitivity. The changes in voice quality and audibility due to the preacher's emotional state are difficult to predict, yet important to the reception of the sermon. I stress the necessity of eye contact when possible with the listeners. Often preachers read the manuscript or look above the heads of the congregation. Preaching *at* someone means one is not attentive to what is going on during the preaching moment. Preaching *with* the people means that there are numerous levels of engagement. Attention to the listeners' oral response and body language informs the speaker of the reception, understanding, confusion, contemplation, or rejection of a sermon. Predictability in delivery, style, and voice is one of the agents of communication interference. It can lead to dull, boring, lifeless, stagnant sermons. The beauty of the human voice is that with little energy, one is able to sound excited about what is being said. The length of the sermon during delivery should be tempered by the attention span of the listener. There are times when the preacher sticks with a prescribed length–10, 15, 25, or even 85 minutes based on traditional understanding of "good" preaching–rather than clear, concise, convicted presentation of God's Word. The performance aspect of preaching is fertile ground for redundancy, rejection, and superficiality. Listeners learn to respond in perfunctory responses rather than question what is being said or not said. If the preacher places himself or herself in the position of the congregation or remembers what did not appeal to him or her in listening to sermons of others, perhaps mute, glib, or trite sermons can be alleviated.

The sermon content includes melding of the selected text, the purpose of the sermon, images, illustrations, and language. The widely read preacher learns to use language that is multilingual, multisensory, multicultural, pictorial, poetic, and vivid. Words have texture, color, movement, smell, taste, sound, and shape. Word choice and usage are vital to sermon construction. The preacher who uses a vast array of homiletical resources–books, movies, Internet, life experiences, humor, stories from children and elders, classical and popular literature, news, current affairs, global events, references from the sermons of others, science, medicine, other professions, cultural fables, proverbs, community sayings, faith testimonies, music, etc.–as supportive information balanced with the irreplaceable biblical text is more likely to deliver an interesting, compelling sermon.

In an age of sound bites and gigabytes, shameless corner cutting, expediency, and instant gratification, preaching is still a significant time investment. One needs time to prepare, develop, compose, and deliver the sermon. Whether one uses a full manuscript or is extemporaneous, preaching is the result of work. It is an arduous task with delayed results. Sermon focus and organization–introduction, purpose, beginning, body, and ending–are part of the communicative intent of the sermon.

In order for the action potential to be sustained, the preacher needs the courage of personal convictions. The preacher should be invested in the sermon and believable. The effective preacher is not lodged in apologetics, personal emotions, or misplaced anger, and chooses any battles wisely. The consistent preacher avoids a delineation of sins while focusing on changing universally negative behavior. Without presenting cognitive dissonance (saying one thing and doing another) or evoking mismanaged expectations (calling on the people to do the impossible), an action-potential homiletic leads the preacher to articulate the viability of transformation in thoughts, behaviors, and actions.

Sociologist S. N. Eisenstadt sets forth fundamental elements of the movement from who we are to who we can become in a classic study on social change.[7] All humans seek some form of transformation. We each face the same general types of problems. The direction, intensity, condition, degree, time, specialization, or differentiation of problems is variable. The relative strength and composition of the collective determine the amount and type of change. "Innovating elites" are change agents. They are able to offer vision and solutions to the problems. These change agents, however, must be aware of the readiness for change, possible rejection of or resistance to the proposed solution, and absence of resources.

Collective or interpersonal transformation occurs when we reach out to others in similar situations and collaborate. An Ethiopian proverb says, "When spider webs unite, they can tie up a lion." Interpersonal transformation, conversion, or change is initially an individual response to a stimulus or situation. This is the preacher's purpose. When one becomes "sick and tired of being sick and tired," one has the choice of staying in the situation, leaving, or working to effect change. The task of the preacher is to understand the "readiness" of the listener to change. Proclaimers of God's Word are obligated to use each opportunity—not just in big chair Sunday morning pulpiteering discourse, but also on every occasion of sacred speaking—to faithfully engage all listeners' belief barometers.

The content of preaching has historically involved critiques of individuals, church, and society. The prophetic nature of preaching addresses what was deemed to be "not of God" and points persons toward life-changing decisions, which are said to meet God's standards of behavior as recorded in the biblical text and revealed to the preacher. We often see only the surface issues. The change agent preacher looks beyond the obvious in both the biblical text and the lives of the people. Knowledge of the congregation is enhanced when preachers spend time listening to the levels of conversation. There is a cultural understanding that one does not divulge the full extent of one's concern. Some issues are too painful to recall or discuss. It is up to the preacher to frame the issue in a manner in which the listener can identify it, understand its impact, and seek transformation. The preacher utilizes lived experience to relate to the congregation. The preacher empathically references the concerns of the congregation by evaluating the landscape of hearts, emotions, minds, and behaviors. Then with care, the preacher assists the listener in looking past the present circumstance to a God-ordained end. The preacher articulates a view of God and the world, which enables the listeners to reconcile the contradictions of life.

One transformational, action-potential, homiletical paradigm I use follows the pattern found in Ezekiel 37. First, there is an *awareness* of the issue. The preacher deconstructs the problem, situation, or actions of the people. What is really going on in the life of the people? What are the history and the life experience of the members of this congregation? What is the social location? Second is the *analysis* of what is wrong. How long has the issue existed? What has been done in the past to rectify the issue? How effective was the action? Why are the situations present? The third point is *allowance* of space to grieve for humanity. How is the pain issue manifested? What is going on behind the pain? How would I act in the same situation? What texts address the issues? Who in the congregation or body of listeners can identify with the text? Fourth is the establishment of appropriate *methods* of resolution, healing, or wholeness (reconstruction). Preachers at times name and address an issue or a situation but give no hint of how to begin the process of transformation. The fifth step is manageable *action* through projection of small-step solutions or goals. The preacher suggests or implies alternative patterns of behavior in response to God's action in the situation and the responsibility of the believer. The sixth and final step is *acceptance* of the resultant metamorphosis and maintenance of the new situation. The awesome responsibility of preaching means that it is the duty of the preacher to filter and refilter the sermon. Attainment of actualized hope is possible for all listeners. The preacher is to confront self and others with the possibility of the realization of God's promise. The preacher presents the realities of life through the hermeneutics of suspicion and examination of the status quo. Noted homiletician James Harris states the following:

> There are enough–indeed too many–proponents of the status quo. This is why there is an urgent need for effective preaching that is truthful, indicting, confrontational, straightforward–a radical simple strategy that will be heard and acted upon rather than alienating–preaching that will challenge and transform."[8]

The possibility of silence in the pulpit is a travesty. The preacher must place himself or herself in the position of the congregation. The preacher must be aware of the lives of the listeners. Needs cannot be met through mute, glib, or trite persons and sermons from pulpits. I find myself telling students that preachers too often leave the congregation wounded, bleeding, and lying in a bed of "why try?"

The challenge of addressing social issues is absent in many contemporary pulpits. I believe that part of the problem is the transitory nature of congregants, the distance between the pastor-preacher and the people, fear of confrontation, separation of the secular/sacred, and belief that there is no need to address injustice–just the spiritual. The true personality of the congregation is often overlooked. They are a collection of individuals with different needs, knowledge, education, careers, histories, memories, Christian experience, family structures, gender, sexuality, health status, economic levels, marital status, and abilities. At times the preacher believes that everyone is at the same level, going thorough the same problems, achieving the same levels of "success," and that "isms" exist only in the church down the street. The hope-filled events of the individual members, the tragic events that affect everyone, the life passages, the celebrations, and the day-to-day living of the membership must be diligently addressed, or the sermon is irrelevant.

This is not to say that one must always address an "issue" or "problem." The preacher is, however, obligated to understand evil in all its forms and power. The dignity of the individual must be preserved. The listeners should have some insight into self-empowerment—the basis for change from negative to positive faith potential. The present situation does not define one's total existence. In spite of the encounter with societal ills, such as racism, sexism, ageism, classism, materialism, or even academic elitism, there will ultimately be an equitable resolution, a healing, a change, or a sense of empowerment for the better. Hope is alive in the preaching that raises critical questions about the lives and lifestyles of all persons. Hope for individual and communal transformation or change is woven into sermons regarding: helping poor and needy; recovery from addictions (sins); giving love; equal prosperity; restoration of relationships, community, and health; end of oppression; end of ecclesiastical apartheid; alleviation of social triage; acknowledgment of another's humanity; and God's granting of eternal life to all believers.

The role of the preacher is to assist the listeners in the identification of spiritual, social, cultural, psychological, and economical issues that impact daily life. The church at times shoots its wounded, then rubs salt in the wounds and proceeds to teach each other to mask pain as if God is an absentee God. The sense of disenfranchisement stagnates personal pursuit of relationships, goals, and objectives. The exhortation in preaching is to inspire, give hope, and declare the eternal watchfulness of a God who never slumbers or sleeps (Isa. 40:28–31). Addressing social and political issues, and outlining social ministries is paramount in the preaching event. The preacher through the sermon seeks to preserve the oral tradition, reminds people of cultural values, instills compassion for all persons, and keeps hope burning in the hearts and minds of the community.

Action-potential homiletics aspires to move past what is and sustains the new state of being for all persons. Resting-potential homiletics ignores the realities of the people's lives, beliefs, and actions.

Action-potential preaching considers local and global concerns. There are preaching universals that contribute to the expectation that life will change for the better. While troubles, difficulty, ostracism, or pain (anywhere by anyone) continue, God's instruments of preaching are obligated to translate the text into opportunities for joy, inclusion, and healing in a not-yet-but-soon-coming reality. Preachers must speak to the deeper needs of the people in worship, presupposing they are taking time to be aware of those needs. Some are so involved in the sermon preparation and delivery, they neglect the persons who will receive it. Preaching is one portion of worship, not the sum total of the event.

The preaching event is open to everyone through God's call, not by a decision of a board, denomination, society, or institution. In the priesthood of all believers, all are welcome to participate in worship and work regardless of age, gender, sexuality, class, ability, or health status. Preaching with global vision means that the preacher accepts the fact that all persons are created equal regardless of creed, color, religion, environment, or culture. In the twenty-first century, the preacher must be relevant. He or she may not have a desire or may not be led to address social issues, but she or he has an obligation to be aware of the problems and questions facing the congregation.

The purpose of preaching is to address the evil that exists in our midst. The pastoral-prophetic preacher also holds a mirror up to his or her life and does theology through speaking repeatedly of our duty to "do justice, and to love kindness, and to walk humbly with God"; keep awake (be diligent); and learn to love God, self, and others.[9] The usual topics of racism, classism, sexism, ageism, handicappism, heterosexism, and militarism come immediately to mind. In the shifting climate of domestic and world events, terrorism, bioterrorism, political repression, new poverty, the AIDS pandemic, welfare, immigration, environmental destruction, conspicuous consumption, and racial profiling demand attention. Domestic violence, cultural imperialism, human rights, crime and punishment, children's rights, alienation (loneliness), right to life issues, religious bigotry, euthanasia, and cultural barriers grounded in linguistic differences are each fertile ground for action-potential preaching. Failure to be aware of any of the topics listed is tantamount to resting potential. The result of the purpose, task, and challenges of preaching is not an overnight, quick fix, name it and claim it reality. It is the repeated retelling of God's presence, power, and purpose in the lives of the people who hear the word of God proclaimed.

Preaching lives up to its purpose and potential when the stereotypes associated with who is a preacher and who cannot be a preacher are obliterated. The word of God is energized when the preacher is prepared to stand in the gap for God and the hearers. Preaching is one of the most vulnerable, time consuming, delayed gratification, and at times misunderstood professions. Jokes are made about preachers only working one hour per week. Challenges of one "being holy" or closer to God abound. The preacher risks public critique of private thoughts, personal beliefs, developing abilities, painful emotions, and individual aspirations. The task of the preacher is to place the word of God and the lives of the people before his or her own during the preaching moment, trusting that God will fill in the gaps. Preaching is enlivened when the preacher is fully, authentically invested in substance over style, passion over performance, pastoral care over pastoral manipulation, and exegesis over isogesis.

Preaching's purpose is to stimulate the people to action. It is to call the people out of arrogant imposition on others and to self-transformation. The hope of such transformation is alive in the preaching that raises critical questions about the lives of all persons. Action-oriented preaching averts annihilation of humanity. Preaching lives up to its potential when the word of God is communicated boldly, clearly, and passionately. The biblical text has been examined, deconstructed, reconstructed, and avoided for centuries. The necessity of persuading people to change preceded the canon.

Twenty-three years ago I taught fledgling speech-language pathologists about the neurological wonders of the human body. Preaching has brought me full circle through an adapted metaphor of action potential. In the neuron the positive charge enters the negative inner cell, and there is an impulse of change across the membrane until the cell takes on a positive charge. This is momentary; the cell returns to the previous negative state, and the process begins again. In preaching the positive energy is represented in the biblical text and the promises of God. The negative charge is the thoughts, beliefs, and actions of the person struggling with faith. The impulse of the Holy Spirit overshadows the negative with the positive move toward transformation. The Word permeates the mental, intellectual, emotional, and spiritual aspects of the hearer.

The person then associates it with his or her desire to change. The change is sustained through constant study of the word of God and the reiteration of the stories of God's plan for our lives. Many people have preached God's Word. In Christianity God inspired the Word; humans now interpret it through God's direction. The contemporary preacher offers a varied perspective on an old, old story.

A so-called "good" sermon is one that speaks to the needs, thoughts, and differences of the listener. The preacher's integrity, willingness to follow the move of God, and the fearless desire to address the needs of the people set the impulse of change in motion. Resting potential means that there is a return to the previous state. Action-potential preaching transcends negativity. It presents the possibility of ending dehumanization and sustaining validation of personhood. Purposeful preaching presents alternatives for life. It points to new directions and sacred spaces for living life as God intends. Preaching's purpose and potential is that the preacher and the listeners go back another way, sustained by knowledge of God's eternal energy transmission.

Alpha, Omega, and Everything in Between

Toward a Postsecular Homiletics

LUCY LIND HOGAN

In the fifteen years that I have been teaching preaching, I have wrestled with developing a succinct, engaging description of preaching that both defines and captures its essential core. One of my colleagues appeals to the aphorism that describes preaching as "one hungry person telling another where to find bread." Yes. That is one of the things we do. But is that all? So, when asked to contribute to this volume and put forward my understanding of the *purpose* of preaching, I was thrown back into this quandary. How would I describe preaching? What *is* the purpose of preaching?

It did not take long to realize that I could not write this chapter without changing the request. I cannot give a *purpose* of preaching. I have come to understand that preachers do not have one purpose, one goal. That is the reason I have not been able to develop the terse description. So, with my editor's permission, I would like to begin by altering the challenge slightly. I will, in this chapter, explore not the purpose, but rather the *purposes* of preaching.[1]

A Particular People at a Particular Time

Preaching begins and ends in God, and in our relationship with the loving God who has created and redeemed us. And, as difficult as it often is for preachers to believe, preaching is an essential part of both our individual and communal relationship with God. We have been called to add our voices to the great cloud of witnesses.

Preaching begins with an individual preacher who has been called. It begins with a group of people, whether it be ten people gathering in a small, rural church on the eastern shore of Maryland, or ten thousand at a "megachurch" in Dallas. And it begins at a particular time. That time might be a quiet service on a lazy Sunday in the middle of August, or it might be the fourth out of six services on a hectic Christmas Eve. While God is the same yesterday, today, and tomorrow, each preaching moment is different, unique, impossible to duplicate. That makes preaching more of a challenge. What worked for one group of people in a congregation at the 8:00 a.m. service will not work for the family service at the same church at the 9:30 service later that same morning. Each moment is new and calling for a new word.

Paul understood that each group of people presented different challenges and needs:

> I have made myself a slave to all…I became as a Jew…I became as one under the law… I became as one outside the law…To the weak I became weak, so that I might win the weak. I have become all things to all people, that I might by all means save some. I do it all for the sake of the gospel, so that I may share in its blessings. (1 Cor. 9:19–23)

In order to share God's blessings with others, Paul realized that what would work for one group would not work for another. The communities, situations, and times were different. Wherever we preach, we are presented with the same array of challenges. One group of people will need to be comforted, another converted. One Sunday they may need to be chastised and challenged, another Sunday, congratulated–"well done, good and faithful servants."[2]

Preachers are called prayerfully and thoughtfully to discern the right word for the right time, words that will build up and strengthen the people of God. The characteristics of our time as preachers include the legacies of modernity and secularism, which have, in part, led to the contemporary milieu of postmodernity. These are challenging times to be a preacher.

In a recent essay in *The New York Times*, Peter Steinfels somewhat jokingly suggests that religious thinkers and researchers might not be so tentative or neglected by the larger culture if they "simply drop that old-fashioned word 'religion.' What they are about, they should announce is 'postsecularism.'"[3] While Steinfels may have had a touch of irony in his article, I agree with his assessment (and appropriate his terminology). In this essay, I would like to analyze two contemporary visions of the homiletic enterprise, both of them in conversation with the concerns of the postmodern situation. I will then discuss a new theological school, radical orthodoxy, and argue that it makes a contribution to a postsecular homiletics, and offers a potential corrective to those initial two visions. In so doing, I propose that this stance ushers in a new vision of a postsecular homiletics—confident and thoughtful preachers using words to communicate faithfully the reality of a living God.

Yesterday, Today, and Tomorrow

I would like to explore the purposes of our preaching by turning our attention to an important and often overlooked dimension of our preaching—time. By that, I do not mean the length of the sermon. Rather, I want to encourage preachers to keep a balance in their preaching among recalling God's mighty deeds of the past, caring for our neighbors in the present, and keeping ever before us the knowledge that our lives and future are in God's powerful and loving hands.

In his work on rhetoric, Aristotle describes three different species or genera of rhetoric; and each, he writes, "has its own time."[4] Judicial rhetoric, the speeches of the courtroom, are focused on past happenings. There the listeners, or jury, are then asked to judge for or against something that has already happened. The rhetoric of the present, *epideictic* or demonstrative, covers a variety of types of speeches—funeral orations, celebratory speeches. And finally there is deliberative rhetoric, the speeches of the democratic assembly, which direct the listeners' attention to the future. The members of the assembly are being asked to judge the future. The speaker urges for or against a certain action, and the listener must decide whether or not to permit or vote the necessary funds.

While Aristotle saw these as three separate and distinct kinds of speeches, I would argue that preachers cannot and should not do that. Our sermons must strive to hold all three—the past, the present, and the future—in a divine tension or balance. Through our preaching, we are called upon always to direct our attention and the attention of our listeners to all three—the past, present, and future, "the Alpha and the Omega, the first and the last, the beginning and the end" (Rev. 22:13). Only then will we have a full grasp of salvation's story.

With that before us, how are we to regard the purposes of preaching? If we hold before us God's time, the alpha (the beginning), the omega (the end), and everything in between, what will a balanced preaching life contain? In the remainder of this essay I will explore what I believe are these essential times and purposes of preaching: the past—formation; the present—the call to mission; and the future—the sacramental dimension.

> *Gloria Patri, et Filio, et Spiritui Sancto*
> Glory to God the Creator, and to the Son, and to the
>   Holy Spirit:
> as it was in the beginning, is now, and will be forever.

As It Was in the Beginning: Preaching as Formation

> How will I benefit you unless I speak to you in some
> revelation or knowledge or prophecy or teaching?
> (1 Cor.14:6)

We cannot locate ourselves in either the present or the future without first turning our attention to the past. To know who we are, we must know where we came from, whose we are.

How can we come to people unless we come teaching them about the Gospel, the wonderful things that our God has done, and the stories of our brothers and sisters who witnessed to God's presence in their lives? Formation, teaching, and pedagogy must therefore be an important dimension of our preaching.

While we may regard Mary Magdalene as the first preacher of the good news of the resurrection, the first formal definition of preaching did not occur for another 1,200 years. In the beginning of his work, *De arte praedicatoria* (*On the Preacher's Art*), written about 1199, Alain de Lille defined preaching as "manifest and public instruction in faith and morals, zealously serving the information of mankind, proceeding by the narrow path of reason and the fountain of authority [Holy Scripture and the writings of the Fathers]."[5]

In his first letter to the church in Corinth, Paul reminds them that, "I fed you with milk, not solid food, for you were not ready for solid food" (1 Cor. 3:2). We must be sure that people are fed with milk, the basics of the faith. They need to have a firm and solid grounding before we move on to the meat of the gospel.

People must be taught the stories and the history of the men and women who went before them. Worship and preaching provide the opportunity to give people "instruction in faith and behavior." It is not enough to wear a bracelet asking, "What would Jesus do?" People must be given the background and resources that will enable them to answer the question. Often we are assuming too much knowledge upon the part of our listeners. We may be feeding our congregations too complex a diet.

My students tell me that one of the most difficult sermons I ask them to write is one written specifically for a "seekers" audience. Although I do not recommend separating out nonbelievers and devoting services to seekers—better that they worship with a community of believers—we must be sensitive to their presence among us. The students are charged, therefore, with writing a sermon that cannot assume any knowledge on the part of the listener. They cannot assume knowledge about the Old or New Testaments. They cannot assume their audience knows the parables and teachings of Jesus. And they must be very careful about their language. We may speak about grace, salvation, redemption, but will our listeners have any idea what we are talking about? It forces the students to realize how many assumptions they make about their listeners' level of knowledge.

Today we are preaching to people who have little or no knowledge of what Alain de Lille identified as "the authorities." Their knowledge of Christ, the Bible, church history, doctrine, or tradition is minimal. And, as one of my colleagues in biblical studies notes, movies provide most people with their knowledge of the Bible and its stories. They think that Charlton Heston is Moses and Willem Dafoe is Jesus. Theologians, therefore, have come to appreciate anew the importance of pedagogy and formation. We cannot forget to teach people about our past.

One group that has turned its attention to the importance of formation are the postliberals.[6] Postliberal theology, as presented by George Lindbeck, is grounded in the understanding that, at the end of the twentieth century, three theological theories of religion and doctrine have both dominated and corrupted theological thinking: the "cognitive propositional"; the "experiential-expressive"; and a third option, favored by Roman Catholic theologians Karl Rahner and Bernard Lonergan, employs a hybridization that attempts (for Lindbeck, unsuccessfully) to combine both.[7] Lindbeck and the Yale school find these lacking.

> As we move into a culturally (even if not statistically) post-Christian period,…increasing numbers of people regard all religions as possible sources of symbols to be used eclectically in articulating, clarifying, and organizing the experiences of the inner self. Religions are seen as multiple suppliers of different forms of a single commodity needed for transcendent self-expression and self-realization.[8]

Rather than a theological theory that understands doctrines as "informative propositions or truth claims about objective realities,"[9] or one that "interprets doctrines as noninformative and nondiscursive symbols of inner feelings, attitudes, or existential orientations,"[10] Lindbeck argues for a "cultural-linguistic" approach in which "religions resemble language together with their correlative forms of life and are thus similar to cultures."[11] In other words, one "learns" to speak Christian the way one "learns" to speak French. "A religion can be viewed as a kind of cultural and/or linguistic framework or medium that shapes the entirety of life and thought."[12]

In his work, *Preaching Jesus*, Charles Campbell examines the significance for and contribution of postliberalism to the preaching enterprise by reviewing the theological/hermeneutical approach of Lindbeck's colleague, Hans Frei. Like Lindbeck, and Barth before them, according to Campbell, Frei argues the inadequacy of orthodoxy and liberalism: "Liberal theology…moves inductively from human experience to theological assertions, in contrast to orthodoxy which (in equally problematic fashion) moved deductively to human life from abstract, external propositions."[13]

According to Campbell, Frei turned to Lindbeck's "cultural-linguistic" model, which views the Christian religion as "a social phenomenon, constituted by the language and practices of Christian communities."[14] When the Christian community gathers together, it tells the story, so that the members learn the content, the vocabulary, and the grammar. For postliberals, "to be a Christian is not primarily associated with having some 'religious experience,' but rather with learning a particular language and set of practices."[15]

The goal of preaching within the postliberal "world" is to "teach" or "form" people into Christians. This is accomplished by telling the stories of Jesus, not because we are to follow the same plot or because we are to tell stories. "Preaching is not primarily storytelling or narrative artistry, but rather an act of moral obedience."[16] And, standing firmly within the Barthian stream, Campbell argues that ultimately, preacher's words are powerless and must depend on God's Word by drawing people out of this world and back into the biblical world which is the only "real world."[17]

The postliberal approach would be seen to argue that all we have is language. However, the language of the postliberal is a restricted one, limited to the biblical narrative, eschewing its truth value and experiential dimension. All we have is language and learning that language—the language of the past. But what happens if we only look back to the past? Do we retreat into isolated, separate communities who have no desire to interact with the world around them?

Is Now: Preaching as a Call to Mission

The church's teaching and preaching, however, are not limited to rehearsing the past. They also direct our attention to the present. We must be clear about situating that present in God's present. Much of today's culture is present oriented—but it is also self-oriented, and we must be careful that we don't confuse them.

At the end of his gospel, Matthew paints a portrait of the final judgment. As the sheep and the goats are separated, the decision is made based on the individual's willingness to offer food to the hungry and drink to the thirsty. People today continue to hunger and thirst for the Word. People may be offered food and drink in the weekly sermon, but, as I mentioned earlier, it is crucial to ask—what are they being fed? We live in an age of super-sized fast food, and much of our preaching today provides calories but no nutrition.

Whether we like it or not, most of us who live in North America live and move in a culture of consumerism. Our market economy exists and thrives in a cycle of need—demand—sales. A business discovers, discerns, or creates a need in individuals, and convinces them to demand the product or service that the business then sells or provides. Do most of us really *need* an automobile that is the size of a small elephant and can drive over rocks and through stream-beds? The largest wildlife I usually encounter are deer not much larger than a Great Dane. And I rarely "ford every stream." But automobile manufacturers spend millions—perhaps billions—of dollars trying to convince me that I will do better and be more successful if I drive their mega-SUV.

Need-demand-sales, therefore, becomes important grammar, and it is easy for preaching to slip into that "language." When we do that, we see the sermon as a "sales pitch." What are people's needs? What are they demanding? The church can meet that need and satisfy that demand. And they will be more successful, happier, more fulfilled if they attend our church. But a sermon is not a "commercial" for the church.

Nor is a sermon a self-help seminar. Another dominant grammar in contemporary culture is that of psychotherapy. Television, radio, print media are all filled with the advice of experts who will help solve all problems. They will explain: how to live with a difficult child or aging parent, how to shed excess pounds (from eating the super-sized fast food), how to manage time so as to be both a loving parent and a success in the business world, and how to conquer addictions of every form. In this culture people come to expect and demand the quick-fix. And they can easily come to view church not as a worshiping community but as a support group.

The consumerist and the therapeutic are two ways to approach the present. But as I have said, they approach the present in the self, in the individual. In his book *The Teaching Sermon*, Ronald Allen observes that, "Christian teaching is helping the community name the world (and its experience in the world) in terms of the gospel...the news of God's unconditional love for each and every created entity, and God's unfailing will for justice for each and every creature.[18] Preaching needs to draw us out of ourselves into the community and into the world.

Yes, our preaching needs to make the past come alive. But preachers must not leave their listeners with the impression that the wonders were wrought only in the past. We may inadvertently leave people with the impression that God has ceased to act in our world.

Although firmly grounded in God's salvific acts in the past, an important purpose of preaching is also to direct the attention of the listeners outward into the present, God's present, and the lives they are living. As Mary Catherine Hilkert observes, preachers are following in the footsteps of Peter (Acts 3:12–26) who "points to the power and presence of God. He names grace...Preaching announces that God has defeated the power of sin and death in the resurrection."[19] And preaching directs people to their responsibility in the world today, for when we name grace it will "deepen their commitment to one another and make decisions that will affect future choices."[20] We cannot solely focus on the events of the past, nor look only ahead to what awaits us in God's future. As preaching awakens us to God's actions in the world, it also awakens us to our role and responsibility in bringing in God's reign and care for the other.

Christine Smith has developed a theology of preaching that lifts up our ethical responsibility.[21] In our preaching, she challenges us, we are to weep with and for those who suffer in our world. Through our preaching, we are to confess how we have fallen short of God's call to us: "If preachers believed that their sermons were acts of confession, they would be pulled back time and time again to the real world in which we live."[22] But weeping and confessing are effective only if they are combined with resistance to the evil of the world: "If preaching is to be a transforming act, then the power and integrity of our proclamations will surely be measured by their ability to mobilize communities to resist the reality that confronts us."[23]

Preaching is about living and acting in the present, in the world of here and now. In a secular world driven by materialism, consumerism, and individualism, the postliberal response is to invite people into a community apart and separated that, as John McClure observes, reads "the Bible in order to foster identity."[24] This, however, as McClure points out, is problematic given that we preach in the shadow of the deconstructionist conversation, which understands words and writing as an endless play or "web of undecidability."[25] We read, and in doing so must necessarily interpret the Bible in an open and never-ending process. But if reading is always indeterminate, how can one form a community around "what Rebecca Chopp calls 'a perfectly open sign'?"[26]

In his book, *Other-wise Preaching*, McClure argues that preaching must take seriously deconstructionism and must seek to import deconstructionist insights into homiletic's ongoing conversation. McClure says, borrowing from biblical scholar John Barton, "the search for the way in which a genre of communication 'always and necessarily undermines or contradicts the philosophy on which its own plausibility relies' in order to keep itself historically alert and open."[27] Scripture, as a text, is therefore always undermining and contradicting. It deconstructs each reading and interpretation, undermining even its own plausibility. Scripture, along with other central homiletical *topoi*—tradition, religious experience, and reason— must, for McClure, be "exited."

Ultimately, as McClure points out, this process of exiting is problematic for preaching because it is grounded in nihilism. When all of the layers are removed, at the core there is nothing. We live, McClure reminds us, "in a culture bereft of true authority, captivated by nihilism." And while McClure argues that preachers must come to terms with the impact this has on their preaching, he realizes that preaching cannot be grounded in "the abyss of nihilism."[28]

For assistance, McClure turns to the philosophical approach of Emmanuel Levinas, a postmodernist who seeks to avoid the plunge into the abyss. Levinas does this by recognizing the centrality of "the other." Awareness of the other brings with it the recognition of an obligation to and responsibility for that other.

Preaching must become aware of the other. It will then become "a saying, that is a sign given to the other, peace announced to the other, responsibility for the other."[29] Preaching is a sign that is always open, always ready for the other. Preaching must therefore constantly work against the tendency toward closure. In order, therefore, for preaching to keep itself "historically alert and open," it must exit "those things that authorize its existence," namely scripture, tradition, experience, and reason.[30]

McClure argues that in the end there is only the other. We do not have a text in the way we have thought of the text before. We do not have a tradition in the way we have appealed to it in the past. And we cannot trust our experiences, nor our ability to reason. Thoroughly and fully grounded only in the alterity of the present, we have only the face of others. But is that all there is?

Matthew reminds us that God has called us to care for and nurture others–to feed and clothe them. But we cannot forget the context in which these instructions are given and who is giving them.

And Will Be Forever: Preaching and the Eschaton

We do not examine the question of preaching's purpose in a vacuum. We all bring to it our own personal experiences and theological understandings, whether firmly established or newly developing. Charles Campbell is seeking to reconnect congregations with their forgotten past, their forgotten foundations. Christine Smith and John McClure are seeking to reconnect congregations with the ignored neighbor.

I know that I, in my worship life as well as my academic life, struggle with trying to unite two very different understandings of the role of preaching. I grew up in the Episcopal Church, in the liturgical, sacramental world that has traditionally been accused of having downplayed the role of the sermon in worship. So, within my church family I have wondered–how can I elevate the importance of the preached word, the sermon in that community? At the same time, most of my students come out of theological and ecclesiological backgrounds that put the sermon in the foreground and downplay the place of the eucharist or holy communion in worship. Is it possible to balance Word and sacrament? Or must one give way to the other?

I would argue that the balance between Word and sacrament is essential, as is the balance among past, present, and future. Our past and our present make sense only when viewed in relationship to God's future, the *eschaton*. The question of whether or not we cared for our neighbor is asked by God at the final judgment. If that is a forgotten or ignored dimension of our preaching we are perilously out of balance.

A challenge to preachers and preaching today is to reconnect us with the transcendent power of God. As theologian Graham Ward observes, in our postmodern culture we are witnessing a "re-enchantment of the world." First, he notes, "a dignity is restored to the emotional and experiential."[31] They are not seen as "contrary to a monolithic reason." Second, he sees that "there is a new respect for what cannot be explained, for that which remains mysterious and ambiguous."[32] And we are seeing that "ecclesiology is seen as central; the community within which love is to circulate is particular."[33]

Ward is a member of a theological school that is seeking to re-enchant the world that has been disenchanted in the wake of modernity. We have already seen two responses. A postliberal homiletic espouses a reconstruction of the biblical world, narrative, and grammar of behavior. On the other hand, a deconstructionist homiletic–distrustful of the metanarratives emerging from tradition, scripture, reason, and experience–turns only to the face of the other. While both of these present important points of view, I would argue that for purposes of preaching these two approaches remain incomplete. Is it possible for the startling reality of Christianity not only to bemoan and react to the disenchantment of modernity, but to address its causes and so begin its healing?

In no way is it possible in this brief essay to present either an exhaustive or comprehensive examination of this complicated school of thought. That would be far beyond the scope of this essay. My purpose is to introduce and make the reader aware of radical orthodoxy and its mode of engagement with the questions of postmodernity. My setting forward of this approach should, in no way, be construed as a wholesale endorsement of this theological school. Rather, I will argue that their theological critique offers a significant challenge to dominant theological approaches and their homiletical conversation partners.

Who and What

Should we call radical orthodoxy a theological school or a movement? Regardless of which term one chooses, this began at Peterhouse College at Cambridge University with the work of John Milbank (who is now at the University of Virginia), and his colleagues and students. Along with Milbank, the principal authors in the movement are Graham Ward, the dean of Peterhouse, and Milbank's doctoral student Catherine Pickstock.

As Pickstock notes in a relatively lucid article describing the movement (one should note that while intriguing, the writing in the movement tends to be obtuse) that it began when a number of people recognized that their approach to theology was taking a turn:

> [W]e had all begun to pursue theology in a slightly different way, and...the already established combination of traditional theology and collectivist politics had begun to assume a new and distinctive form...To the mix of orthodoxy and political radicalism had been added, by a new generation, a third ingredient, namely postmodernism.[34]

Out of this interesting–and somewhat unlikely–mix has come a theological approach that sees the "nihilistic drift of postmodernism" not as a portent of doom, but rather as an opportunity. While the principal proponents of this school have authored a variety of texts in which they have gradually developed their key themes,[35] they recently co-edited a text in which they seek to synthesize the major themes of their emerging theological approach.[36] It is from the introduction of this collaborative work that I have drawn the description of their approach.

They observe that while too many theological movements of the past century have tried to either "shore up" sagging theological approaches or "baptize" postmodern approaches in the light of contemporary critiques of religion, radical orthodoxy "seeks to reconfigure theological truth [with a] proposal of the rational possibility and the faithfully perceived actuality, of an indeterminancy that is not impersonal chaos but infinite interpersonal harmonious order, in which time participates."[37] At the center there is not "nothing"; there is God. "Everything participates in God; meaning is open-ended but not drifting in a void; we trust that we are being led above ourselves to a vision we cannot yet attain."[38]

They make the claim for orthodoxy in that they remain committed to the ancient creeds of the church. But more than that, they see in their claim to orthodoxy a commitment to "reaffirming a richer more coherent Christianity which was gradually lost sight of after the late Middle Ages."[39] They do this with a methodology that seeks to combine exegesis with cultural reflection and philosophy "in a complex but coherently executed *collage*."[40]

They identify themselves as "radical" in the sense that they seek to return to the patristic and medieval roots. In particular, they seek to lift up Augustine's vision "of all knowledge as divine illumination."[41] In doing so, they want to argue against the modern dualisms of faith and reason, and nature and grace. But even more significantly, they see themselves as *radical* in the more contemporary understanding of that word. They seek to challenge and criticize "modern society, culture, politics, art, science and philosophy with an unprecedented boldness."[42] While they may not necessarily be "manning the barricades," they do see themselves as promoting not a postmodern or postliberal Christianity, but rather a post secular Christianity that "is led to articulate a more incarnate, more participatory, more aesthetic, more erotic, more socialized, even 'more Platonic' Christianity."[43]

What does the critique of radical orthodoxy contribute to the debates in contemporary homiletics? While more topics could be discussed, I will highlight three that I view as key insights: the doctrine of participation, the relationship between faith and reason, and the resurrection of the sign premised on the doctrine of transubstantiation.

Participation

According to Milbank, Pickstock, and Ward, the "central theological framework" of radical orthodoxy is participation. By that is meant the Christianized platonic understanding that all life, all creation, all matter, all culture, all language "live and move and have their being" in God. Because everything is created by God, everything shows forth the glory of God. And to say that there is a separation between the things of the world and the things of God is to "reserve a territory apart from God," which is impossible.[44] All creation is begun and ended in the mind of God, and therefore all creation serves to reveal something of the nature of God.

It was in the Middle Ages, with the writings of Duns Scotus and later that of nominalist William of Ockham that, according to the radical orthodoxy, everything began to go awry:

[F]irst, people started to think that one could talk adequately about the content of things without reference to God...Secondly,...[h]uman beings, in the image of God, began to be thought of as autonomous wills, and human society began to be seen as a college of isolated atoms.[45]

Radical orthodox thinkers seek to heal this fissure, to reunite the material and the spiritual, the body and the soul. We are created by God; we participate in God; and we, and all of God's creation, share in the resurrection. Unlike modern and postmodern philosophy that is caught in a nihilistic fascination with destruction and death, Christians therefore understand that they are not trapped or defined by nothingness. Rather, they know that "if bodies are seen to participate in God, they have eternal significance, and are seen in the light of their resurrection."[46]

Faith and Reason

The proponents of radical orthodoxy betray their Anglican roots in their preference for "both/and" theology rather than the "either/ or" predilection of most other Protestant theologians. An important part, therefore, of their theological agenda is to mend the rift between faith and reason. This dualism, they argue, is a logical conclusion of the trajectory that was established by Dun Scotus and William of Ockham. The vector of this trajectory led to the autonomous realms for faith and reason, theology and philosophy, and, in the wake of the Enlightenment, a progressive diminution and marginalization of the former and the ascendancy of the latter.

As Pickstock notes in her defense of radical orthodoxy, much of contemporary theology has pledged its allegiance to one camp or the other. Liberal theologians find themselves somewhere in the camp of reason. And conservative or neo-orthodox theologians stress faith.[47] Radical orthodoxy seeks to bridge this gap introduced by medieval nominalism. It does so by stressing the participation just described, recovering an earlier sensibility. Milbank writes:

[I]n the Church Fathers or early scholastics, both faith and reason are included within the more generic framework of participation in the mind of God: to reason one must be already illumined by God, while revelation itself is but a higher measure of such illumination, conjoined intrinsically and inseparably with a created event which symbolically

discloses that transcendent reality, to which all created events
to a lesser degree also point.[48]

Resurrection of the Sign/Transubstantiation

Ultimately, radical orthodoxy is grounded in worship, especially
the eucharist. Radical orthodoxy argues that only with a sense of true
ritual do we have a sense that we come from God and give ourselves
back to God. More specific, and perhaps more controversial, is the
claim Pickstock makes about the eucharist and language.

Pickstock traces the lineage of the death of the sign from
nominalism through Derridean post-structuralism and finds in it a
nihilism, even a necrophilia, which is typified by "the sophistic,
modern and postmodern refusal of liturgical life."[49] It is just this
deconstructionist vacuity of the sign that is the exigency for McClure's
exiting to the other. Pickstock proclaims a resurrection of the sign:
"I shall now argue that…it is possible to restore meaning to language,
and that the optimum site of this restoration is the integration of
word and action in the event of the Eucharist."[50] Pickstock stresses
the realism of the real presence of the resurrected Christ in the
eucharist and argues that this undergirds the possibility of meaning
of signs in general: "The words of Consecration 'This is my body'
therefore, far from being problematic in their meaning, *are the only
words which certainly have meaning, and lend this meaning to all other
words.*"[51]

Living between the Alpha and the Omega

Words of praise, celebration, and thanksgiving are the words of
worship and the words of the preacher. When we as preachers and
as a community speak these words, we are connected to the great
cloud of witnesses who have gone before us, and to those who are
seated at the great heavenly banquet. The past, present, and future
merge into one time, *kairos*, God's time, not human time. When we
eat the bread and drink the cup, we are given a foretaste, a glimpse
of the great feast we will someday taste; and we are reminded that
all that we are, all that we see, all that we do are the Lord's. Liturgical
anamnesis, bringing the past into the present, and *prolepsis*, bringing
the future into the present, "constitute," as Laurence Hull Stookey
observes, "a primary means by which we maintain contact with past
and future, both so integral to our identity and sense of mission in
the world as a people of the resurrection."[52]

The sacramental, then, is neither antithetical nor incidental to the purposes of preaching. Rather, a recovery of the sacramental allows a convergence of past, present, and future in a way that can address the anxiety of contemporary homiletics as it responds to the postmodern situation. It reminds us that the biblical world we engage is none other than the world of grace in which we live and whose trajectory is the eschaton. It reminds us that when we turn to the other, we encounter the Other as well. It is this Other who has loved us from the *alpha*, the beginning, will love us at the *omega*, the end, and continues to love us in between.

6

Preaching and the Redemption of Language

JOHN S. MCCLURE

Among the many purposes of preaching is this one: *to speak what cannot be spoken.* Positively, this means we proclaim that there is a holy and righteous God; that this God loves the entire world; that God has redeemed the world through the dying and rising again of Jesus Christ; and that we can live each day delighting in both *torah* and gospel as we look forward to the future establishment of God's reign of justice, steadfast love, faithfulness, and shalom. This is our positive proclamation of the kerygma without which preaching could not take place at all. If a preacher does not claim at least this basic purpose, then there is nothing to say that really matters.

I began, however, by saying that these things "cannot be spoken." What do I mean by that? Here we confront the "negative" side of proclamation, by which I do not mean "negative" in the pejorative sense of "bad" or "less than." Negative, rather, means "negating" and refers especially to a particular ethical "negation of a negation" (transformation) that has preoccupied many homileticians in this generation. The "negation" that must be "negated" is, in one manner of speaking, the capturing and enslavement of words and symbols by the principalities and powers. This negation has engaged many homileticians in this generation with a new purpose for preaching. This purpose, we might say, is the *redemption of language.*

Following in the footsteps of Isaiah and Jeremiah, T. S. Eliot, the great modernist poet, reminds us that, in the presence of the holy God, all our words

> *strain,*
> *Crack and sometimes break, under the burden,*
> *Under the tension, slip, slide, perish,*
> *Decay with imprecision, will not stay in place,*
> *Will not stay still.*[1]

In fact, in this postmodern generation, words have come unhitched from any stable reference point altogether, and tend to say more about other words and the use of those words than about the mysterious reality that is the focus of proclamation. We no longer assume that the meaning of a word or symbol is a simple matter of finding its standard dictionary reference, or that meaning will be ontologically "disclosed" by the word or symbol itself. We now know that meaning comes largely from the ways that words are used within groups and societies. This has had the effect of making us very aware of issues of power, and especially abuses of power, in relation to language. In other words, we have become sensitized to the ways in which the meanings of words are a function of their *use*, and this has made us wary of the ways that words are often *mis*-used.

Another way of saying this is that, more than any generation before us, we are keenly aware of the ways in which the principalities and powers can invade and co-opt the very language we speak. French novelist and literary critic Maurice Blanchot points out that a post-Holocaust world threatens to destroy living, communal speech and writing.[2] We in North America know only too well how easily words can be used in support of the destruction of life. Even the words of faith can be used in this way. Many preachers in the South during the civil rights movement used the pulpit to support violence against blacks. For centuries, women have found themselves shoved into the margins by the bully pulpit. These are two of the more prominent instances of the destructive use of language in the pulpit. Many more occur every Sunday. This situation requires that we give special attention to the business of *redeeming language.* I suggest that this requires at least two responses from us as homileticians and preachers: (1) that we learn to speak the language of *resistance;* and (2) that we learn how to speak the language of *love.*

Preaching as a Language of Resistance

First, as Christine Smith points out in her book *Preaching as Weeping, Confession, and Resistance: Radical Responses to Radical Evil,* we must learn to speak the language of resistance, of prophetic assertion.[3] This is the language of refusal and reclamation, in which the potentially violent references and rhythms within our common language are taken to task, exposed for what they are, and reshaped or re-scripted. The work of Walter Brueggemann, in particular, has been helpful recently as preachers consider what it is to de-script congregational and cultural discourse, and to re-script it in a way that is faithful to the cadences, grammar, and purposes of the scriptural Word.[4] To coin a word, preachers are in the business of "re-languaging" people's lives. They deconstruct dangerous meta-narratives and replace them with narrative fragments that might become the building blocks for a new discourse of righteousness and peace.

Another, more subtle aspect of this resistance, however, relates less to the *content* of discourse than to its *embeddedness* within unredeemed inter-human structures. The human language-function itself seems to feed off the defensive, survivalist elements within the human psyche and within social consciousness. As Ana-Marie Rizzuto and Ludwig Binswanger have shown, when a child is born, the child screams first "words" to defend against perceived threats and in order to attach itself to something that will provide immediate safety and comfort.[5] The same dynamic occurs at a social level, where language is used to shore up social boundaries and to attach us to that which will secure us against perceived dangers. This quality of language is easily co-opted by the would-be idolatries that offer to secure people on a daily basis, especially consumerism, militarism, and various phobias. This defensive aspect of language wants to attach us to what will secure us, and to repel that which is perceived as alien or "other."

At an even more subtle level, Louis Althusser and Jacques Lacan have demonstrated that part of the trickery and deception of language within the larger social setting is the way it creates a mirroring process, whereby the dominant ideology "hails" or calls to us as individuals and groups and creates an image for us of who we are. Antonio Gramsci developed this idea further with his idea of *hegemony*, the process whereby "common sense" is established according to the interests of a dominant group within society. This common sense includes those values, beliefs, practices, and forms of knowledge that "go without saying." These things that "go without saying" constitute a hidden language that is scripting all of our lives. As preachers and homileticians, we know now that we are not only up against potentially dangerous everyday uses of language, but we are also up against certain dangerous elements within this massive silent social grammar.

Primarily, we are up against a certain "double bind" that exists in the way that hegemony as a silent language asserts itself. Let me try to summarize this process briefly. The center (hegemony, dominant ideology) requires the margins in order to be the center. This creates a double bind because the struggle against the center paradoxically props up the center. The lived experiences and language of everyone within its scope always make sense from the vantage point of this all-defining center. This elicits a struggle for survival by those at the margins. At the same time, it elicits a sometimes violent response by the center in order to "keep the margins at the margins." Both of these dynamics make it nearly impossible to deconstruct and re-script this deep cultural language that "goes without saying."

As the Church begins to experience itself less at the center, less a part of that which "goes without saying" in our world, and more at its margins, an unusual opportunity for Christian preaching emerges. If we pay attention, we may stand to learn a great deal from all marginalized people within society. They have a great deal to teach us, not only about the ways and wiles of the dominant ideology, but also about the way the proclamation of the gospel has always meant *Jubilee* ("freedom for repair") from the violent rhythm that exists between this dominant ideology and the margins. This homiletical *Jubilee* could be one key to unlocking this double bind and creating a new space within language in which to plant and grow new linguistic structures and meanings.

As homileticians and preachers, therefore, it is likely that we will be learning a lot in the years to come from the proclamation that has for centuries been taking place among marginalized people, especially African Americans and women. In particular, we will be learning from those for whom "testimony" is the core meaning of proclamation. By testimony, I do not mean "personal testimony," at least not exclusively. Testimony is a powerful speaking out of the context of one's own life, but it is done on behalf of an entire community who are struggling for identity and for the acknowledgment and reception of its traditions of interpretation and meaning.

Making use of Rebecca Chopp's theology of the Word, Anna Carter Florence asserts that preaching as testimony can break this violent rhythm between hegemony and its "others," by *sealing* the preacher's speech to a Word that is a "perfectly open sign."[6] Referring to women's testimonial speech, Florence asserts that "our lives are not the testimony, and our lives do not prove the testimony; rather our lives are *sealed* to the testimony, sealed to the narrated and confessed freedom the testimony proclaims: the Word as perfectly open sign."[7] In other words, we can learn from marginalized traditions of preaching the necessity to "testify" in a way that seals our preaching to a Word that is a "perfectly open sign," i.e., a Word that is absolutely free from the violent rhythm that exists between hegemonic speech and its "others." It is this *Jubilee* quality of proclamation that Jesus was calling to our attention in the synagogue (in Luke 4) when he read the *Jubilee* text from Isaiah, and then he proclaimed that this Word was "fulfilled" in their hearing.

African American homileticians have also drawn attention to the fact that preaching can break apart this violent rhythm between the center and the margins. These homileticians accentuate the absolute freedom that springs forth from hearing this liberating Word, a freedom that marks the "celebration" within many traditions of black preaching. According to Henry Mitchell, this celebration emerges from a deep "internalization" of and "saturation" by God's liberating Word (cf. Florence's "sealing").[8] This internalization becomes what Warren H. Stewart calls "an awareness that God is involved in one's wholistic liberation."[9] Olin P. Moyd asserts that this experience is literally "unstoppable."[10] Testimonial speech of this type will be very important in coming years as preaching attempts to break our language free from the vice grip of this center-margin double-bind.

We have a long way to go in pursuing the language of resistance in preaching. Brueggemann, Chopp, Florence, Stewart, Moyd, Charles Campbell, and others have made excellent progress so that the way forward is now clear. I anticipate that, as preachers and homileticians come into further conversations about how to achieve these goals in the pulpit, even greater strides in this direction can be made in the future.

Preaching as the "Signing" of Love

The second purpose of preaching, as it seeks to redeem language, is for preaching to become the language of love. To some extent, learning this language begins with an experience of the preacher's own expressive disaster in the midst of the co-optation of language by the powers. According to Blanchot:

> It is upon losing what we have to say that we speak–upon an imminent and immemorial disaster–just as we say nothing except insofar as we can convey in advance that we take it back, by a sort of prolepsis, not so as finally to say nothing, but so that speaking might not stop at the word–the word which is, or is to be, spoken or taken back. We speak suggesting that something not being said is speaking.[11]

Preaching can harbor a separate language that is other-wise to any language that we can speak verbally. This language exists just beyond the threshold of the preacher's experience of the disastrous inadequacy of language and the complicity of language in potentially violent, oppressive cadences within discourse itself. This separate language, we might say, is the language of love. It emerges within our face-to-face *proximity* to the others around us, in the sanctuary and in the world. Just beyond the prophetic re-scripting of discourse, and beyond the testimonial sealing of our preaching to the "perfectly open sign" of God's Word, there can emerge within our preaching a largely passive language through which preaching becomes a "signing" to others, a "saying" to others of our proximity, our mutual exposure and vulnerability to each other.[12] Preaching that expresses this language begins to speak *agape*.

This agape-language is a direct extension of the *Jubilee*-celebration of the "perfectly open sign" in preaching. It is a byproduct of the infinite "otherness" that invades preaching when it is sealed to this Word-sign. It works, in part, like this. The preacher attends closely to each face in the room, but also sees through these faces to other faces and then to others, and so on. In this way, an infinity of "others" begins to enter the room, an infinity whose presence is welcomed in by the *Jubilee* of the "perfectly open sign" in our midst. In other words, as *Jubilee* is announced, a "signing" of love begins. This signing speaks, without language, of infinite responsibility (ethics) and of infinite compassion (love).

Preachers can learn to attend to this silent language, the language of love. It is true, as Blanchot points out, that this language withdraws from other languages. It is satisfied to exist as a *signing*, a cipher that cannot be spoken unless it is "taken back" lest it be co-opted by the larger system of language. It is crucial, however, that we begin to think about preaching as a passive act, or signing, of love—of our love for each other and God's love for us. This, and only this, can ultimately redeem the language that both rages and dances between us. Ultimately, loveless power within language usage can only be reclaimed by love itself.

How can preachers learn to express this love? The question might be posed in this way: How can preachers make their preaching a truly welcoming, face-to-face experience? These are questions that have been occupying the minds of many homileticians, including Christine Smith, Nora Tubbs Tisdale, Lucy Rose, Chuck Campbell and Stanley Saunders, Kathy Black, Ronald Allen, Susan Bond, and others.[13] In each instance, preaching is embedded deeply within some form of mutual speaking-listening, face-to-face interaction, whether conversation, encounters on public streets, congregational study, the inclusion of personal testimonial speech during sermons, or a deep attention to the many strangers within a congregation whose lives are seldom raised to the level of speech, including persons with disabilities, the aged, those who have been victims of sexual or domestic violence, and many others. The assumption is that the language of preaching will work to redeem language as a whole when it emerges within redemptive practices of proxemics, or face-to-face speaking and listening.

Once again, there is a long way to go if we are to invite *agape* fully into our pulpits. What are the implications for performance and delivery? What are the larger ethos issues that are involved? What other kinds of practices (peacemaking, hospitality to strangers, etc.) need to subsume or supplement the act of preaching? What does this mean for character ethics and preaching? What does a homiletical theology of love look like? There are signs that some of these issues are beginning to be addressed, as homileticians find their way toward these problems and seek to address them. As they do, and as preachers hone the various models already at work, it is possible that the language of love will become a central component of preaching in the new millennium.

Conclusion

We return, then, to consider our brief excursus into the question of the purpose of preaching. We have said that one positive thing, the kerygma, has to be pursued, and that one negative thing, the redemption of language, has to be pursued. Our positive purpose is, as always, to faithfully proclaim the message, the kerygma, without which we have nothing to say. Negatively, our purpose in this generation has been to consider how it is that we can reclaim the common languages that we speak and our symbols of faith–to release them from the clutches of the principalities and powers that have bound and double-bound them in ways that ultimately breed distrust, alienation, and violence. Positively, proclamation requires boldness and faithfulness to the message of redemption in Jesus Christ. Negatively, proclamation requires the *Jubilee*-language of resistance and the "signing" of love. Only with both our positive purpose and our negative purpose well in mind can we proceed to consider and reconsider each component of the preaching process, from the early stages of preparation to the closing "amen."

Preaching

Hospitality, De-Centering, Re-membering, and Right Relations

CHRISTINE SMITH

Asking the question, "What is the purpose of preaching?" feels a bit like asking the purpose of poetry or the purpose of film, theater, art, sculpture. Preaching is such a holy, expansive craft and art form, how could one ever answer the question as if preaching has only one reason for being? Preaching is such a contextual act, responsive to the needs, longings, joys, and concerns of particular communities of faith, how could one answer the question abstractly or theoretically? Preaching has everything to do with the preacher, the proclaimer, the one who bears witness. How could one answer the question without understanding the particularities of the preacher?

Over the past several decades, preaching has gone through revolutionary and radical changes, placing even greater and more wholistic expectations on the preacher and on the preaching event. As preachers and teachers, we have experienced the liberating movement away from deductive, linear, propositional preaching toward inductive, evocative, transformative preaching. Those of us who teach craft urge students to learn how to craft their sermons in ways that invite individuals and whole communities into experiences, into meaning, into truth, into holy encounters that will leave people nourished and changed. Today we no longer hope preaching will be engaging and experiential for preacher and congregation alike; we *expect* this to be true, and we strive for this reality.

So, "What is the purpose of preaching?" A part of this homiletician feels cautious about writing from this vantage point, for fear of stepping back into deduction, back into a posture of preachers somehow deciding what is to be "distilled" from written biblical texts and life experiences, that then can be "applied" to people's lives of faith. The question, as powerful and important as it is, may threaten to violate the changes many preachers now embrace and celebrate. Even though the question leaves room for a multitude of responses, it may have some implied "shoulds" and "oughts" that might perpetuate clerical domination and lead us to think too narrowly. Even though one may try to "break out" of any of the constrictions implied in the question, I still find myself thinking I should name *one* major, essential purpose and then make a case for its importance. I am resisting this temptation. In fact, I want to start with a *prior* question before moving toward "the purpose of preaching."

Over a decade ago when I taught at Princeton Theological Seminary, the team of preaching professors opened the basic preaching course each semester by addressing a very different question. We each spent ten to fifteen minutes addressing the question "Why preach?" This question feels more vulnerable, more passionate, more urgent, more compelling. This question invites the preacher and the homiletician to bear witness to the power of the act of preaching; to confess (speak truthfully about) its enduring value; and to testify about one's deepest religious hopes and visions for this act of ministry.

Why do I preach? I preach because there is need and there is gift. I preach because the needs of human beings and the needs of our created earth cry out for redemptive, salvific religious responses in words and in actions. In addition to critical life and death needs, I preach because I believe in the grace-filled presence and power of a liberating God. God's presence is sheer gift—and constantly with us—enabling our own work of creation, redemption, and liberation. I preach because I experience my life claimed and called by this One who gave me life and calls me to bear witness to life. It is the presence, power, and possibility of God, my relationship with God, and my relationship with all creation that calls forth my preaching.

Preaching is a theological act, one in which preachers are called to reflect on the mysterious nature of life, trying to discern and proclaim the nature of the divine, the nature of human existence, the nature of the divine-human relationship, and the nature of human responsibility in relation to all God's creation. It demands the skills of a very articulate communicator, the attentiveness of a sensitive biblical and textual exegete, and the social analyses of the most discerning sociologist. One is never a theologian in the abstract, or in general. One does theological and religious work out of a matrix of social realities that constitute much of one's being.

My social location is an important part of "why" I preach. As a European American, highly educated, able-bodied person of enormous economic and social privilege living in the United States, and as a woman and as a lesbian, I seek to preach in ways that urge people to feel, speak truthfully about, and resist injustice and oppression of all kinds. The dual realities of being complicit in oppression, and directly experiencing oppression, are a very important part of what compels me to preach.

Because I understand myself as a liberation theologian, and thus preach and teach out of that perspective, I view preaching as first and foremost the craft and act of a working theologian, committed to religious community, and committed to the transformation of an unjust, oppressive world. Liberation theology is a theological understanding and methodology that begins with the lived realities of oppression in our world, and seeks to move toward the liberation of the most oppressed and marginalized in our world. Liberation theology has molded me in a very significant way into the particular preacher I am, and has shaped the commitments out of which I preach. Preachers become increasingly believable and honest the more they are able to articulate their social location and social context, and to understand how these realities influence everything they do in the act of preaching.

Why do I preach? I preach because preaching is an act of public theological naming. It is nothing less than the honest, bold, fearful interpretation of our present world, and an eschatological invitation to a profoundly different, new world. In the preaching act, the preacher has the responsibility to offer a taste, a vision, a glimpse, of the "kingdom" of God; and to bear witness to places of life and resurrection in the face of a world in which death, inflicted suffering, and violence of every imaginable kind threaten to rule. I preach because this life is possible, and I believe that faithful preaching participates in this uncompromising commitment to life. Preaching cannot be bound by a Trinitarian formula, yet it clearly and unabashedly is an act of creation; it has the potential to sustain life, hope, and promise; it can participate in the redemption and transformation of reality.

For me, only after naming some of the reasons I preach am I able to move to some of the many purposes of preaching. But once again, how can one answer this question in the abstract? Preaching is utterly contextual, and the contexts in which it happens shape and call it forth, and require different words and different embodied acts. Maybe the question is best approached by moving more into the artistry, the story, the movements that have changed the heart and soul of preaching in recent years and let those things once again reveal to us the many layered purposes and possibilities of the task and craft itself. In some ways, why would we answer this question any less evocatively, any less indirectly, any less experientially, or any less transformationally than we craft our sermons? Maybe the question is best answered by locating oneself in contexts that reveal what preaching and proclamation are all about.

> Life, life is what you must affirm, no matter how painfully, even unwillingly...You are reliable only when others ascertain they will always find life in your presence. Others must know you as faithful, faithful so often that when they wonder where life lives, they will think of you as one in whom life has made a home.[1]

Being invited into the worlds of people in whom life has made a home might just lead us into some of the purposes of preaching. Experiencing and being changed by people who affirm life, no matter how painfully, just might remind us again "why" we preach.

March 18–April 3, 2002–Chiapas, Mexico

I have come to be immersed in Chiapas for sixteen days. I have come to learn, to explore possibilities for immersion in theological education, to be changed. For decades in the state of Chiapas, there have been many powerful movements for change and liberation. I have come to realize that the Roman Catholic Church in the Diocese of San Cristobal de las Casasis profoundly influenced by the prophetic voice and ministry of Bishop Samuel Ruiz; the active nonviolence of "Las Abejas"; the ongoing struggle for life by the indigenous people throughout Chiapas; and the Zapatistas, are all a part of movements for change and liberation here. The strategies and beliefs embodied by those who are working for change in Chiapas are varied, sometimes radically distinct and even in conflict with one another. It is a complex place, difficult for me to fully understand, and yet a place of great religious faith and a place where liberation theology has taken root in many life-giving ways. I am recalling at this particular moment an essential part of the history of this place, and the message of life and liberation it proclaimed to the world.

The Zapatista Movement is an indigenous civil rights movement. It began in the early 1980s; and since that time the Zapatistas have worked steadily throughout the years for justice, liberation, and dignity for the indigenous people of Mexico, particularly those in Chiapas. I am remembering that on January 1, 1994–the same day that NAFTA, an economic agreement that has had devastating ramifications for the poor throughout Mexico, was to take effect–the Zapatistas rebelled. This was an international movement to act on behalf of thousands of people of Mayan descent, throughout Chiapas, who suffer and die daily because of global economic and social policies. They shouted to the world that day, "Ya Basta!" or "Enough is enough!"[2] And from that day until this present moment, they are still saying, "Enough." They are demanding justice, democracy, and freedom for all people, especially the most oppressed indigenous people of Mexico.

The Zapatistas made a bold statement to the world on behalf of life, yet Chiapas is filled with people and communities, each in their own right, who are seeking justice, and creating "home" for life. It is in the context of this ongoing struggle for liberation, justice with dignity, and life that I am reminded, in powerful and indicting ways, why we preach and, hopefully, some of the purposes preaching serves.

March 28, 2002: Maundy Thursday–The Roman Catholic Church in Amatenango, Chiapas, Mexico

We arrive early, before the Maundy Thursday worship service so we can spend some time with Paty, a pastoral agent and lay leader of this church (part of the Roman Catholic Diocese of San Cristobal de las Casas), and Carlo, an Italian priest who serves this church and the larger parish of which it is a part. I have come to this holy place with Rev. Delle McCormick, a United Church of Christ pastor who has been serving as a person in ecumenical mission with the Diocese of San Cristobal in Chiapas for almost two years. This town and parish are places of special importance in her overall ministry in Chiapas. I arrive as guest; she arrives as beloved pastor and religious leader. Carlo Celli, Paty Camacho, and Delle McCormick are a pastoral team in this holy place of cultural dignity and violent oppression. Most of the people of Amatenango are of Mayan descent and speak Tzeltal. They struggle for survival and liberation in the face of a global economy that starves and kills them on a daily basis, and renders them as "disposable" human beings. They are a proud and strong people, in the midst of a long legacy of racism against indigenous people in Mexico and throughout the Americas that seeks to strip them of all human dignity and ethical agency.

After I am introduced to Paty and Carlo and we visit for a few moments, Delle and I walk quietly into the sanctuary to prepare for the service. We stand against a side wall. I am unsure where I am to be, or what I am to do. Delle has worked hard to earn the trust of the people in this community. The trust she has developed enables me, a complete outsider, to be invited into this place. I am greeted with unspeakable warmth and acceptance even though my country, and I as one of its privileged citizens, directly participates in the oppression of each person who enters the church that day. I am keenly aware that we are two European Americans, two Protestant women pastors in the midst of a completely indigenous Roman Catholic religious community. Further, we are large people compared to the indigenous women and men who live in this community—an immediate, visible sign of the horrible malnutrition of a whole people and of the overabundance in my own life. I feel awkward and uncomfortable. Across the front of the sanctuary is a huge wall of beautiful flowers I have never seen before. The table is set for holy eucharist, and white candles burn throughout the church.

Much could be said about the worship service that unfolded. Three sacred acts etched a permanent mark on my heart and soul: a ritual of blessing and sanctification, an act of radical inclusion and empowerment, and a ritual of humility and justice.

The elders of the community are first to enter the church. These are older women and men who come quietly into the church and take their seats on simple wooden benches. The older women sit on one side of the church, the older men sit on the opposite side. Delle and I are standing and watching the elders enter. As we are waiting, the women of this religious community insist that we take two of the precious bench seats, knowing very well there will be many women who will stand throughout the service. It is wonderful to have a seat, yet it is horrifying to be granted such unearned privilege once again in my life.[3]

After the elders are seated, all the "younger" members of the community come into the church. As they enter, I feel the palpable power of the younger women going up to the older women and the younger men going up to the older men, bowing their heads to be touched on the head–a blessing freely given to them by the beloved, respected elders of their community. It is beautiful to watch; but at the same time, it is a painful, terrible reminder that something profound is lacking in most of the religious contexts I have experienced. This is a ritual of blessing unlike any I have ever seen or known. I find myself feeling empty inside. What must it feel like to show this kind of respect to one's elders in the context of religious community? What must it feel like to receive a blessing from them? I have never witnessed a deeper or more profound sacramental generational act.

The service begins. I know just enough Spanish to understand some of what is being said. At other times, when Tzeltal is spoken, I simply do not understand what is being said. I am lost in a world that is not my own, yet strangely familiar with many of the embodied Christian gestures and rituals I have known all my life.

I watch and listen carefully. An indigenous woman reads the scripture, Paty proclaims the homily, and women serve the elements of bread and wine. In a world where women are still violated in every conceivable way, treated as property, and rendered insignificant and unimportant, the women of this community are preachers, teachers, and sacramental agents, at least for a moment. All these women are doubly oppressed by their ethnicity and their sex. The boldness of their words, the honesty of their social and religious analysis, and the proud humility of their service are overwhelming. Visually, I feel shock at how often Carlo stays seated, and I am keenly aware of just how silent he is for much of the service. Instead of asserting the most power that he might assert, it appears to me that with great intention, he is stepping aside, stepping back, so that others may exercise their long denied voice and religious power. The women's power and voice, as well as Carlo's posture and silence, become in those moments icons for me of what is possible and what is just in the Christian church.[4]

The third act is one I have witnessed and participated in throughout my life of faith, yet I could never have been emotionally or spiritually prepared for what then begins to unfold. At the appointed moment in the service, Carlo takes a basin of water and a towel and walks toward twelve of the male elders and religious leaders of this church. Carlo, an Italian priest dressed in the simple yet privileged garments of clerical status, bends down on his knees, washes the feet of twelve indigenous religious leaders, then kisses each man's foot with great humility and care. It would sound too wonderful to say I am crying tears of inspiration, even though this is true. At the same time, I am overcome with grief. How can it be that I have spent my whole life in the Christian church and never witnessed this kind of "foot washing"? Without trivializing any single time I have washed people's feet and had my own feet washed, I know in an instant that I have never seen the dirty, dusty, hardworking calloused feet of the most marginalized of the world, of indigenous people throughout the globe, washed by a person of authorized, institutional, religious power. This is radical enough. Then he bends over and kisses each man's foot. I am stunned in the wake of this mighty act of servanthood and justice. I weep, struggling hard not to wail out loud. This is more than a taste of God's commonwealth here on earth.

What is the "purpose of preaching"? I am not sure. What I do know, with absolute certainty, is that this Maundy Thursday service in Amatenango, Chiapas, embodies what preaching must be about. Worship and preaching must be about sacramental honoring and blessing. With words, images, and embodied acts, preachers need to remind us to bow our heads to receive the blessings of community; and then to humbly take our seats beside, or humbly stand behind, those who have birthed us and sustain our lives with wisdom, endurance, and courage. By "de-centering" ourselves from places of power and faithfully limiting our constant access to "voice," preachers need to empower and be silenced by the voices of those who have little voice, and even less power. Preachers need to enable people in every context of life to notice those most marginalized and oppressed; preachers then need to consciously step back as those who have been disempowered take the bread of life and the cup of blessing into their own hands, as they are the ones who feed and nourish their own communities of faith.

Perhaps most importantly of all, preachers in all contexts of institutional Christianity—and those of us in countless contexts of unearned advantage and privilege—need to be the kind of interpreters of scripture, the kind of sacramental agents, the kind of religious leaders who take up the honorable and needed mantle of liberating servanthood.

May our sermons bring us and the people of faith with whom we share life to our knees, ready and honored to wash the calloused feet of those who are suffering and those we oppress; and may our preaching be inseparable from our justice acts of kissing feet.

In the Roman Catholic Church of Amatenango, life has clearly made a home. It has made a home as indigenous women, men, and children, and a pastoral team of a mestiza lay woman, a European American United Church of Christ woman pastor, and an Italian priest mutually accompany one another through daily moments of life and death. It has made a home in health care providers, and the women's and human rights promoters. It has made a home in the life-giving blend of traditional Mayan blessing and ancient Christian foot washing. It has made a home in the words, gestures, acts of humility and respect that are found in this place called "church," and the ways it nourishes and sustains those who struggle for daily survival. It has made a home here because, for more than forty years, the people of this diocese have worked in a steady, committed way for the rights and liberation of the indigenous people. Life is here because religious people have had a persistent commitment to resist the politics and practices of death, and an equally bold commitment to the politics and practices of life for the most marginalized.[5]

March 31, 2002: Easter Worship–Acteal, Chiapas, Mexico

Delle McCormick and I are making our way from San Christobal to Acteal. As we drive higher and higher, and with each dramatic curve in the road, I am aware that I am about to spend Easter with a people who know, in their bodies and in their communities, the absolute violent reality of crucifixion and the profound hope of resurrection. Delle and I are talking about the Abejas; she is rehearsing some of their story.

Over the years the government has coerced and manipulated many indigenous people in Chiapas to take up guns against the Zapatistas, pitting indigenous people against one another. The Abejas have refused to submit to this inhumane betrayal. They have refused to take up arms against the Zapatistas. They, too, are of Mayan descent. They speak Tzotzil. They live in many villages throughout the region of Chenalhó. Primarily Roman Catholic, they are a highly organized civilian association committed to active nonviolence and alternative economic practices that sustain life.

The Abejas (the "bees") are like bees in nature for they, too, have a queen bee. For some of them it is the organization itself, united and working for the justice and peace of the people. For others, "Christ, and those who are Christ's representatives and leaders in the world" are the queen.[6] The Abejas have refused to take up arms against the Zapatistas. As a result, the government has inflicted military intimidation and violence upon them. The violence became so great between September and December in 1997, many of them fled from their villages, leading some to settle temporarily in the town of Acteal. They were displaced people, refugees, fleeing military and paramilitary violence. They are hardworking people, most of them farmers and artisans trying to live peacefully and faithfully with their neighbors.

In Acteal, on December 22, 1997, sixty armed men dressed in black fatigues attacked and opened fire on a large gathering of the Abejas who were gathered in a chapel fasting and praying for peace. They killed twenty-one women, fifteen children, and nine men. Five of the women were pregnant.[7] Crucifixions happen each and every day; and this one happened three days before Christmas to members of a community who had faithfully stood their ethical and religious ground. They continue to symbolize and embody the hope and promise of reconciliation, and peace with justice. Their powerful, peaceful resistance in the face of retaliation, oppression, and death is an act of unbelievable fidelity.

We will be worshiping this day with the Abejas in and around Acteal. I have never spent Easter in a place of such crucifixion!

We arrive in Acteal, park the car, and walk down the mountainside toward the center of Acteal, a village that clings to the side of a mountain, tenuous but sure. As we get closer, we see hundreds and hundreds of people. Many of them have been on a Holy Week pilgrimage walking from village to village all week long, only to end their pilgrimage here in Acteal on Easter Sunday. The priests who will celebrate mass, indigenous deacons, religious lay catechists, members of this religious community, and a small but obvious group of international visitors are there. When we first arrive, we see many, many people walking slowly around what is known as the Pillar of Shame. It is a "sculptural outcry," depicting tortured, screaming women, men, and children. Intertwined throughout the sculpture are various reptiles and a large snake, symbolizing the beginning of time when animals and humans came from a common trunk.[8] We join in and spiral around it three times. After this essential ritual act, all those who are gathered begin to make their way down a hillside.

As we walk, several women are carrying the remains of a wooden carving of Our Lady of Guadalupe that was in the chapel when the massacre happened. It was disfigured during the shooting. They have placed it in a special case, and this is a central part of the procession. There are men carrying religious banners. All of us make our way into the place that has been prepared for morning worship. It is an open air chapel, with a plastic roof, a simple communion table, wooden benches, and a few chairs. Delle and I take our seats on a bench at the back of the chapel. We wait. When all is ready, visitors come forward, introduce themselves, and speak a word of greeting. As I leave my seat to go forward, I feel sick; I cannot say in Spanish what my heart feels, nor do I know one solitary word of Tsotsil. The imperialistic arrogance of knowing only English has never been so obvious and indicting. After each one of us speaks what we can, people clap, and celebrative music plays. I cannot remember a time when I have felt more humbled, or more honored. Every time the Abejas worship, they include this ritual of welcoming visitors. It is a generous act of hospitality, and it is a humble act of thanking people for not "forgetting them." I will not forget.

The rest of the service unfolds. New indigenous male deacon candidates and their spouses are commissioned for special leadership in this religious community. They come forward. An older couple from the community who has served in this way presents each new couple with a simple wooden cross. The parish priest of Chenalhó, Pedro Arriaga, is officiating. At one point in the service, he specifically invites and urges a woman to speak. In a place where women seldom speak in religious ceremonies, an indigenous woman rises to her feet to share a testimony of faith. There are forty-five tall candles attached to a wooden board, and each is lighted to remember each of the forty-five people who were massacred. I am aware throughout the service that a woman sits close to the candles, tending them while fanning incense.

Music and singing permeate every movement of the service from beginning to end. There are no clerical robes here; rather, the priests are wearing the same Mayan clothing as all the indigenous men who are leaders in the church and community. All the male leaders wear colorful hats distinct to the Mayan heritage of the indigenous men. The priests sit among the people. Spanish is spoken. Tzotzil is spoken. Babies are nursing; and the wonderful, life-filled noises of children hum in the background. We are invited into "strong prayer." All of us collectively kneel and speak aloud to God what we hope and expect God to do. It is powerful, it is holy, it is strong. It is prayer that assumes God will respond, empower, and act.

The offering is carried forward and placed on the table. There are offerings of candles, beans and corn, flowers, incense, and water. Communion is served. Each person is invited to partake. No one is excluded from the table. The indigenous deacons and their spouses serve the elements. For three hours we share Easter life here. There is no rushing, there is no hurry. Ritual moments unfold with grace and ease, with a complete lack of pretense and a distinct kind of reverence. This is worship, the work of the people, where all are invited to speak and move, and to act as one mighty witness.

We end this part of the service in this particular space, and then we process down the hill and quietly walk into another building. It is the tomb of the forty-five people massacred in Acteal. We enter at one level and see several steps downward to another level. Delle and I, along with many others, stand on the upper part. The priests, the survivors of the massacre, and others fill the lower space. In this holy space members of the community stand alongside the martyrs who have died rather than above them. Together we feel the spirits and the resurrected life of those who have died in our midst. We remember and re-member them. The martyrs' names are spoken, and all proclaim together, "They live with us."

The official service ends. People quietly leave the building. I linger long enough that I find myself alone. I walk to one side of the building, read each and every name of those killed, and look at their pictures. At the other end of the building I read the beatitudes placed there, each with a picture from contemporary life. I stand there in that tomb reading in Spanish, "Fortunate are those who mourn, for they will be comforted. Fortunate are the meek, for they will inherit the earth. Fortunate are those who hunger and thirst for righteousness, for they will be filled. Fortunate are the peacemakers, for they will be called children of God."[9] I walk down the steps to the lower level and feel rage, sorrow, grief, and shame. Finally, I make myself walk out of the building and join the community meal that is happening. It is a shared meal of *caldo,* broth with a small piece of chicken, and tortillas. I sit quietly as I eat my meal. Because I speak only a little Spanish, and no Tzotzil, I am not even able to speak with those I am sharing life with around this table. I am overcome and overwhelmed. I have never spent Easter in a place of such resurrection!

What is the purpose of preaching? I am not sure. What I know with absolute certainty, however, is that this Easter Sunday service in Acteal, Chiapas, embodies what preaching must be about. With our words, images, and embodied acts, preaching must take a stand for life in the midst of violent crucifixions. Preaching must enable people to create and honor "sculptural outcries," and to have the courage and commitment to preserve a dismembered Our Lady of Guadalupe. Preaching has to do with Holy Week processions that gather the community together in prayer, in witness, and accessible tables where all God's people are welcome. Preaching is about people sharing a simple, nourishing meal together after emerging from a tomb. It is about speaking words—and inviting words to be spoken—that will nourish and sustain a community to hold fast to their religious and ethical beliefs in the midst of violent repression. It is about "Las Abejas" speaking about forgiving those who perpetrated the massacre only one day after it happened, while simultaneously calling for justice. It is about a mestizo priest being invited to turn away from the clerical garments of church hierarchy and power, and instead wear the dress of those whom he serves. It is about an entire community's understanding the power and promise of standing alongside the earth that holds the remains of their loved ones, instead of standing above or on top. Preaching is about remembering and not forgetting. It is about the kind of "offerings" that remind us we are made of the same substance as earth, wind, fire, and water. It is about a radical kind of grace that embraces and celebrates the presence of "outsiders"—even outsiders from the United States—who benefit in many ways from our nation's economic policies, yet directly and indirectly participate in the very violence that killed beloved family members. It is about complicit outsiders being changed, and returning to work for change in their own countries. It is about expectancy and hope. Somehow all that is said and done this Easter morning will hold accountable those who need to be accountable; will sustain those who need to be sustained; and will give those who need to grieve and weep the space and holy invitation to grieve and weep. It is about life.

In Acteal, and in the work of the Abejas, life has clearly made a home. It has made a home in the dispossessed, displaced, and most oppressed who refuse to compromise their ethical and religious convictions even unto death. It has made a home in the lives and witness of the Abejas as they returned to their home villages and continued to be agents of active nonviolence. It has made a home in priests who use their power for peace with justice, not privilege. It has made a home in women who participate as religious agents with their prophetic voice and their service to the larger community. It has made a home in the lives of this parish where more and more indigenous deacons are commissioned in the face of the prohibitions and racist mandates of Rome. It has made a home in a tomb where people shout to the world, "We will not forget!"

What is the purpose of preaching? I am not sure. What I do know with absolute certainty is that it has to do with everything I experienced and learned in Amatenango and Acteal. There are so many things I felt and learned and experienced, yet in this final summary section I want to lift up four things that seem particularly poignant and important for the preaching task and for the purpose of preaching. One is about what allows us to preach; the remaining three observations are clearly about its purpose.

Preaching as Hospitality

My experiences in Amatenango and Acteal taught me once more that worship and preaching emerge as a result of hospitality and invitation. Rereading the words I have written describing both of those contexts, I realized that preachers preach because of the graciousness and the hospitality of the community. This is the starting point of preaching. It should never mean that this invitation gives any community the right to control, manipulate, or compromise what preachers ultimately feel they must say and do in the preaching act. Yet, it is an act of graciousness extended by the community that could easily be assumed or taken for granted. I believe the priests and the women preachers in both contexts knew just how much hospitality has been extended to them. They responded by being bold and prophetic. May the invitation to preach bring forth prophetic boldness in contexts of great oppression, and contexts of great privilege.

Preachers, and those who teach preaching, often spend a great deal of time talking about what allows them to preach, or what gives them the "authority" to preach, and what kind of "authority" the preacher possesses. In 1989, in my book *Weaving the Sermon: Preaching in a Feminist Perspective*, I offered a critique of this word. I suggested that for many women—particularly women with a feminist, social justice consciousness—the question of "authority" is not the primary or appropriate question to ask, and certainly is not the word we would use to describe what allows us to preach, and what is at stake in the act of preaching. In that book, I suggested that many women would not talk about preaching as a special right or privilege that one earns somehow with degrees or clerical status. Rather, preaching is more about a quality of presence, mutuality, and integrity, all of which lead to a kind of intimacy of connection with those one worships with that might just lead to true solidarity and accompaniment.[10] I believe this critique of "authority" so much more strongly thirteen years later.

In Amatenango and Acteal preachers do not preach because they have some institutional authority, for even though the priests in both contexts have levels of institutional power, many others preach. Preachers in these two contexts do not preach because the hierarchy of the church has bestowed some kind of special privilege upon them, for the institutional church has in so many ways completely failed the people and is still trying to control who has the opportunity and power to speak, and who must remain silent. Rather, preachers who preach in Amatenango and Acteal preach because they have been given a sacred gift. They preach because they have been invited to preach. They are invited to proclaim what rises up from their lived experience, from their hearts and souls, from their longing to share a word of life with the community they love.

This is true for all who preach, lay and clergy alike. We are invited to share a word of promise, hope, indictment, and challenge by the larger community who not only accepts our words, but invites and "counts on" our prophetic and life-giving proclamations for daily sustenance, nourishment, and for their own struggle for life and human agency. The words of Henry Mitchell, a prophetic African American preacher and teacher of homiletics, have always haunted me: "There is a radical difference between listening to an essay designed to enlighten and listening to a Word desperately needed to sustain life."[11]

In Amatenango and Acteal preachers offer their words to people who "desperately need a Word that will sustain life." It is the integrity, honesty, and intimacy of this truth that is at the heart of the preaching act in these communities. It is very humbling to know that, as a preacher, the one true thing that allows you to speak is the gift of hospitality given to you by those who receive your words. If individuals and whole communities did not choose to listen, choose to receive, choose to be present to our words, there would be no preaching. If individuals and whole communities did not experience the preacher's words and acts as having integrity, truthfulness, and life-giving power, the meaning and purpose of this act would be rendered meaningless.

De-Centering

Authority did not allow the women to preach and speak in Amatenango and Acteal; rather, it was the act of "de-centering" on the part of the priests, as well as the gracious invitation and receptivity of the whole community. And in faithful response to that invitation, preachers in both cases attempted with humility and great honesty to preach words that would not just "enlighten" but would sustain life.

In Amatenango and Acteal one is reminded again, and reminded in some new ways, that life-giving preaching is about the radical act of "de-centering." De-centering is the act of choosing to relinquish unearned power and privilege, or having it removed on behalf of justice.[12] Whether power is removed for the sake of justice, or willingly relinquished, for people of power and privilege it is an experience of less power, less privilege, and an experience of using what power and privilege one has more humbly, more appropriately, and more in the service of justice. Preachers need to take seriously the power and privilege they have been given to speak religious words that create, sustain, and redeem. Preachers need to understand anew that it is an act of urgent justice that they use this power to enable the most powerless, the most marginalized, the most oppressed, to take back the life-giving human power and agency that has been stolen from them. Preachers who have privilege need to understand more profoundly that "de-centering" is not just something that happens in places of obvious and blatant oppression, but something that needs to happen in every human context, for in every human context there will be people who have had voice and agency stolen from them.

In contexts of great marginalization and oppression, preachers who have privilege need to remain seated and in the background while the most oppressed read scripture, serve communion, serve, and minister, and rise to speak a word of challenge and indictment. When invited and given the sacred honor, they need to wear the clothing and learn the language of those whom they serve. They need to invite those who never speak to speak, and they need to kneel down literally and kiss the feet of the most dispossessed. In contexts of great privilege, preachers need to take greater risks, be bolder and more courageous in their prophetic denouncements and proclamations. They need to listen more and speak less. They need to speak words and use power in ways that put their jobs at risk, place them in positions where they feel out of control in the face of another's world of human difference, and feel humbled and overwhelmed about what they do not know.

For people who are accustomed to always speaking, or at least having the opportunity to speak, and for people who typically have experienced their embodied lives as having unlimited access into places and spaces of all kinds, the experience of being "de-centered" can feel strange, chaotic, overwhelming, and powerless. Preachers of privilege need to learn that these feelings are a sign of essential relinquishment, a sign of greater mutuality and respect, a sign of appropriate humility and gratitude, a sign of justice. It can be an essential transformative experience for preachers of privilege to experience not knowing where they are to be, not knowing what they are to do, not being able to speak the language of the people, and being extended hospitality not because one has power or position, but simply because one is human and has been invited into a sacred place. For people of unearned advantage, privilege, and power, de-centering is a profound act of justice. It has everything to do with each time the powerful choose to preach bravely, choose to listen rather than speak, and choose to be vulnerable enough to be "redemptively lost."

Remembering and Re-membering

What is the purpose of preaching? In addition to the radical act of urging those of unearned advantage and privilege to "de-center" themselves from violating power, Amatenango and Acteal remind me that preaching has everything to do with remembering, and "re-membering."[13] In Acteal, the martyrs are named and remembered by engaging in powerful communal liturgical actions; and participating in communal words spoken, thus, the whole community of Las Abejas is "re-membered." This act of re-membering happens on the twenty-second of every month all year long.

Preaching surely has to do with claiming for the first time, and claiming again and again, that which has been unjustly silenced and stolen. It is about "re-membering" the community, particularly in relation to the most marginalized, the most silenced, the most oppressed. The Abejas do not just "refuse to forget"; they actively and consciously remember each and every person who was murdered by economic, social, military, and paramilitary violence. The act of "re-membering" those whom the world would like to forget is a very radical act—a very faithful, redemptive act.

Preachers need to become increasingly aware of all parts of the "body of God,"[14] and the "body of the community" that have been forgotten and rendered invisible, disposable, severed, unnamed, disappeared, and annihilated. In every community of faith in which preaching happens, from the most oppressed to the most privileged, the body of the community needs restoration, reparation, and "re-membering."

As preachers we "re-member" the body of God and the body of the community each time we are brave enough to speak the names of those most dispossessed. We "re-member" the body each time we claim the most marginalized as our sisters and brothers, and declare that they live with us. We "re-member" the body each time we invite the voiceless in our midst to read scripture, preach a prophetic word, and bear witness to the realities of their lives. We "re-member" the body each time we challenge and urge the powerful to bend down to kiss the feet of the oppressed with humility and respect, each time the eucharistic table does not separate us but brings us together in a common struggle for the commonwealth of God.

This task of "re-membering" is not to be taken lightly. Preachers of privilege must constantly look for those who have been forgotten, silenced, violated, and killed. What might happen in our Christian communities if we were to remember/re-member Yom HaShoah, Holocaust Remembrance Day, in our worship life and in our preaching each spring? What words of understanding and support might we speak about the Palestinians in the midst of so much anti-Arab sentiment in the United States and in so many of our churches? What words of repentance might we speak on Columbus Day for the millions of Native American people who were annihilated and removed from their land?

It is essential that preachers find the courage to speak words of mourning and confession as we speak each year about "Thanksgiving." How might our communities see themselves differently if each year communities across this country re-membered the internment of thousands of Japanese Americans in concentration camps within our own borders during World War II? And during the weeks of February when this nation celebrates the history and culture of African Americans, how might the violence of white supremacy be altered if we re-membered the concrete human conditions and realities of slavery in the United States, and how the remnants of that slavery still continue? There are so many displaced, disappeared, broken, and severed members of the body that need to be restored and re-membered.

Remembering and re-membering will require a very critical hermeneutic as we approach the biblical texts that give rise to our sermons, as we live and as we analyze our daily lives. It means we will spend our lifetimes asking ourselves horrible, yet redemptive questions: Who is not here, and how can they be brought into the body fully and justly as God intends? Who is not listened to, or who has been silenced, and how might we enable their voices not only to be heard and known, but how will our preaching enable those voices to change us and the world of which we are a part? Who has been severed from the body, and how have we been complicit in that severing; and what confessional acts of repentance and reparation must we engage in to restore the body to its God-intended wholeness? With words, actions, and concrete symbols, what will we place in the center of our communal lives that will serve as "sculptural outcries"; and how will our actual sermons be "verbal and spiritual outcries" that lead us to restoration, mending, and re-membering?

On the pillar of shame in Acteal, these words are written: "A sculptural outcry. This sculpture has been erected to denounce the encroachment of the Mexican State on the indigenous population. May the victims be remembered and honored forever; and may the perpetrators be brought to justice and tried for the crimes against humanity." Re-membering is about denouncing all things that destroy and violate the body. It is about making present those who might otherwise be lost and forgotten. It is about creating and re-creating the wholeness of the body in everything we say and do. It is about demanding justice for those who have been dis-membered.

Right Relationship

A final essential lesson from my time in Amatenango and Acteal is this: One of the most profound purposes of preaching is to create, protect, and nurture right relationship. In many ways, all that precedes this section has everything to do with right relationship. Embodying gestures of profound humility; "de-centering" the powerful from places of unearned advantage and privilege; inviting the voiceless and those who have been silenced to proclaim their religious truth and witness; re-membering the wholeness of God's body and the body of the community; proclaiming words that nourish and sustain life; the grace of hospitality and invitation; the commitment never to forget injustices done, violence perpetrated– these are the substance and content of right relationship.

Yet there is more to be said and learned about right relationship from the people of Amatenango and Acteal, and from the transformational experience I had in those places and have sought to share in these pages. In this section, I want to step back from the experiences I had there in order to raise a few crucial questions about the process of right relationship in which preachers engage week after week after week. In this section I have more questions to raise than answers to give, more soul searching to be shared than neat, final assertions about the purpose of preaching. Fundamentally, if preaching is to be about right relationship in content and in process, it must be about actions of accountability and care, rather than actions of appropriation and consumption.

In every preaching class I teach, we speak about the "human faces, the faces of the reality of our world" that preachers include in their sermons. One of the ways preachers talk about this aspect of preaching is to use words, images, story, and imagination to invite individuals and whole communities into "worlds" of meaning and experience. In recent years homileticians and preachers alike have come to appreciate that these faces are more than mere illustrations of a point; they *are* the point, the meaning, the substance of preaching. Whether it is the human face and reality embedded in the biblical texts that give rise to our sermons, or the human face and reality from the contemporary world in which we live, meaningful, life-giving sermons are about human faces, lived experience, God's presence, and life. Yet how the preacher relates to these "human faces," these portrayals of reality, is a matter of serious ethical concern.

Who gets to do the inviting, and whose worlds are we allowed to enter? Are there worlds we simply should not enter even as invited guests? Who gets to name, and with what kind of precision and care will that naming be done? What and whose interests are served by the stories we share, the experiences to which we bear witness, the assumptions we make? How will human differences be honored, not trivialized; truthfully described, not romanticized; carefully shared, not exploited? Who gets to interpret, and who is left out in the interpretive process?

These questions, and many more, need to make their way into the preaching process from beginning to end. As I reflect on my time in Chiapas, I recall my preparations. Even though I could have done so much more, I did read, I attended a class, and I had countless conversations before I ever stepped foot in Chiapas. And once in Chiapas, I went into communities with someone who had worked there for almost two years. Central to right relationship is the awareness of each and every time one is guest, and doing one's own work to try to understand and educate oneself about the realities in which one will be immersed.

How long should we study something, learn about it, watch it, read about it, before we write or speak about it? Maya Angelou, one of the great African American writers of our day, speaks about a woman in New York, a "maid" whom she watched for more than a year. She studied her movements, her laughter, her gestures, her life. Then, and only then, did she decide to write a poem honoring that woman's sense of survival and human agency.[15] This testimony of Maya Angelou ought to shock many of us who are preachers. Before we invite communities of faith into lived realities in our sermons, do we study that reality for a long, long time, sincerely trying to experience a person, a sacred place, a holy ritual in its own right, hoping and praying never to distort or misinterpret? For preachers of privilege, power, and access, I fear so many of us simply assume it is our right to tell, our right to name, our right to interpret. We may not be as accountable as we can be to the sources of our naming, accountable to the individuals and communities that "people" our sermons, accountable to the sacred stories and moments into which we are so graciously invited and are clearly guests.

In the writing of this article, every question I have just raised has surfaced again and again. Perhaps I have violated the ethical standards these questions raise as I have told the story of my experience in Amatenango and Acteal, or at the very least violated some of them. I have tried to minimize the violation, as I cannot avoid it altogether. Every detail of the two experiences I have shared has been checked with people who live and work in those two communities. As I have checked those details, I have discovered many mistaken interpretations, and many things that have deepened my understanding. At every turn, I have found myself truly wondering whether or not a "guest" can ever share sacred experiences of other people without participating in the consumption and use of those people's lives. Perhaps that question ought to be so fundamental to the preaching task that we ask it of every story we tell, every experience we share, every truth we claim, every interpretation we make, every moment we choose to reveal. Right relationship is never about consumption and use. It is always about people remaining subjects, not objects. It is always about "guest" interpreters being accountable to the people and realities they interpret.

The experiences I had in Amatenango and Acteal are clearly just that, *my experiences*. At the same time, they were experiences of such social and religious inspiration—and terrible challenge—that they must be shared. They are experiences that remind me of why I preach. They are experiences that powerfully reveal some of the most important purposes of preaching. It is my hope that both the experiences shared and my reflections upon them will enable preachers of privilege to engage in radical acts of de-centering and in wholistic acts of re-membering the body of God and the body of religious community. I hope that preachers will recommit themselves to deconstructing clerical authority, and embodying hospitality and humility. And finally, I hope that preachers will keep learning how to tenaciously hold themselves accountable to creating and sustaining right relationship in the content and process of their preaching. If, in the craft and act of preaching we do just some of these things, we will open up greater places within our lives and ministries for life to make a home.

8

Keeping in Touch with God
Why Homiletics Is Always
More than Method

THOMAS H. TROEGER

In Touch, Out of Touch

When I was ordained in 1970, someone gave me a reproduction of Michelangelo's painting of the creation of Adam on the ceiling of the Sistine Chapel. God, lying upon a bank of clouds, extends a forefinger toward the forefinger of Adam so that they are just barely separated. My reproduction of this famous icon of Western art varied in only one way from the original. It featured a cartoon balloon coming out of the mouth of God with the words: "Keep in touch."

I have long since lost the reproduction, but the words have stayed with me. Keep in touch with the source of every good and perfect gift, keep in touch with the animating energies of all that lives, keep in touch with the deep dear core of things, keep in touch with the power of justice and the grace of compassion, keep in touch with the one who creates and sustains us, keep in touch with the risen Christ, keep in touch with the Holy Spirit—this is the primary mode of being and doing to which preaching calls us.

The Bible has two perspectives on keeping in touch with God. One perspective suggests that it is impossible to be out of touch with God. The psalmist asks, "Where can I go from your spirit?" (139:7) and discovers that no matter where we go, we find God there. Luke, imagining how the apostle Paul would have preached to the Greeks on the Aeropagus, draws upon a Greek philosophical poet and describes God as the one in whom "we live and move and have our being" (Acts 17:28). Paul writes in Romans that when we do not know how to pray, God prays in us through "sighs too deep for words" (Rom. 8:26); and Paul is utterly convinced that nothing in all of creation can separate us from the love of God that is in Christ Jesus our Lord. The writer of Colossians quotes a hymn celebrating that Christ is the cosmic reality through whom all things were made and in whom all things hold together.

The cumulative impact of these passages is to suggest that we can no more be out of touch with God than a bird flying through the sky can be out of touch with air or a fish swimming through the sea can be out of touch with water. We are always in touch with God.

But the Bible also features an entirely different perspective. We are often out of touch with God. Sometimes it appears that God has left us. There are psalmists who cry out in desperation, "My God, my God, why have you forsaken me?" (Ps.22:1) and, "How long, O LORD, will you forget me, forever?" (Ps. 13:1). But other times it is we who have lost touch. The prophet, speaking for the Holy One, observes: "This people worship me with their lips, but their hearts are far from me." And Mark begins his gospel with the announcement that God's reign is at hand and we need to "repent and believe in the gospel." The primary meaning of *repent* is *to turn around,* so that the word implies we are headed in the wrong direction and need to change course. We have lost touch with God and are called to reestablish contact.

Saint Augustine, in his *Confessions,* offers a prayer that powerfully captures how we are both in touch and out of touch with God.

> *O Beauty so ancient and so new...*
> *you were with me,*
> *and I was not with you.*

The purpose of preaching is to illuminate this essential paradox of human existence: our simultaneously being in touch and out of touch with the source and sustainer of ourselves and everything that is. Preachers draw power from their conviction that the "Beauty so ancient and so new" is in touch with human beings. Preachers draw passionate concern for human beings from observing how they have lost touch with that Beauty. Preachers who have enduring credibility are those who acknowledge that they themselves participate in the paradox of being both in and out of touch with God. The primary condition for becoming an effective preacher is not homiletical technique and method, as helpful as these may be, but is rather a willingness to acknowledge and struggle with humanity's paradoxical relationship to God.

The Special Challenge of Technology's Illusory World

Sometimes tragedy or the loss of a world of meaning puts us out of touch with God. That has been true in every period of human history, but I believe our electronic world creates illusions about communication and communion that pose special problems to keeping in touch with God. We think of our era as the most advanced age of communication that ever was:

- cell phones
- voice mail
- laptop computers
- instant message services
- Internet
- e-mail
- cable television
- satellite telecommunications

These have created the illusion of better communication, but in fact they have often only made us more accessible to one another across greater physical distances, while the communion that results from genuine human interaction has declined.

I remember when I was in the airport and my name was called over the loudspeaker. Talking with an agent, I discovered my mother had suffered a severe stroke and I needed to call her physician long distance at once. It used to be that I could have gone into a phone booth, closed the door, sat down, and conversed in privacy. But now I was reduced to using the last phone in a bank of phones that were about ten feet from a television blaring a story about someone who was about to attempt the longest bungee cord jump in history from a bridge over a gorge in Australia. I could barely hear the physician at the other end of the line above the television and the chorus of fellow phone users beside me plus all those talking on their cell phones. It came to a point where the doctor, realizing what I was up against, simply shouted over the line to me, "Just get here as quickly as you can." The human connection that is an essential part of keeping in touch with God was nearly destroyed by the broadcast noise and the telephone chatter.

In a similar manner I recall worship services during which cell phones have sounded. One time the phone's signaling device played the opening to the *William Tell Overture* while we were praying for people who had died. The worship connection that is an essential part of keeping in touch with God was all but destroyed by the intrusion of the cell phone.

I also think of attending a play that built to its most climactic scene at 9:00 p.m. The hour had nothing to do with the drama, but I know it was 9:00 because of the chorus of electronic watches beeping as the heroine realized the devastation of her life. The artistic connection that is an essential part of keeping in touch with God bowed to the disruption by unnecessary electronic beeps.

I recall these stories as one who is on line every day at work and who is grateful that my wife can call me on her cell phone when she is out alone at night. It is not the electronics alone that are a problem, but the way we view them. They create a lack of spiritual awareness that is very close to Saint Augustine's lament:

> *O Beauty so ancient and so new...*
> *you were with me,*
> *and I was not with you...*

Of course, there are many other things besides the illusions of technology that can lead us to Saint Augustine's poignant realization. Sometimes we might wonder during a church meeting how we can keep in touch with God and one another when the agenda looks longer than eternity. And sometimes when we turn on the television or open the morning paper, we wonder how we can keep in touch with God and one another when the sea of bitterness runs so deep. All these realities can put us out of touch with God, and preachers cannot afford to ignore the impact of these forces on themselves and the people to whom they preach.

The Human Genius for Resisting Grace

But once we have allowed for some of the unique factors and characteristics of our age, we who preach need to confront a more profound, more perennial reason why human creatures lose touch with the source of every good and perfect gift. For there is a reality more stubborn and deeply ingrained than the illusion of salvation by technology, or the intractability of church meetings, or the terrors of our age. It is what I call humanity's genius for resisting grace. It is our brilliant ability to find a detour around God even when God is the one in whom we live and move and have our being.

> *O Beauty so ancient and so new...*
> *you were with me,*
> *and I was not with you...*

Augustine's prayer suggests that the problem lies in the depths of the human soul: God is with us, but we are not with God. Or to put it more precisely, our being with God is an on-again, off-again affair, a highly unstable condition. Denise Levertov captures the character of our relationship with God in a poem titled "Flickering Mind."

> *Lord, not you,*
> *it is I who am absent.*
> *At first*
> *belief was a joy I kept in secret,*
> *stealing alone*
> *into sacred places:*
> *a quick glance, and away–and back,*
> *circling.*
> *I have long since uttered your name*
> *but now I elude your presence.*
> *I stop*
> *to think about you, and my mind*
> *at once*
> *like a minnow darts away,*
> *darts*
> *into the shadows, into gleams that fret*
> *unceasing over*
> *the river's purling and passing.*
> *Not for one second*
> *will my self hold still, but wanders*
> *anywhere,*
> *everywhere it can turn. Not you,*
> *it is I who am absent.*
> *You are the stream, the fish, the light,*
> *the pulsing shadow,*
> *you the unchanging presence, in whom all*
> *moves and changes.*

> *How can I focus my flickering, perceive*
> *at the fountain's heart*
> *the sapphire I know is there?*[1]

Finding the Springs of Living Water

How do we who are preachers focus our flickering minds? How do we who are preachers perceive at the fountain's heart the sapphire we know is there? How do we who are preachers keep in touch with God? This question takes precedence over every technical question in homiletics. Of course, the art and methods of creating and delivering sermons matter. If they did not, I would not have spent twenty-five years of my life teaching and writing about them. But what I have observed from listening to hundreds of preachers is this: The most artfully crafted, the most theologically sound, the most beautifully delivered sermon falls dead if the preacher is not in touch with God.

To ask how we keep in touch with God is to ask where we find the springs of living water that feed our heart and mind. I find the metaphor of the spring to be perhaps the most common one used by preachers when they go through a difficult time in their preaching. Preachers will say, "My spring has run dry." Conversely, when they sense the Spirit at work in them and their homiletical imaginations are rich and full, preachers will report how their springs are really running. The metaphor of the spring has deep and ancient roots in the Bible.

> *Happy are those*
> > *who do not follow the advice of the wicked,*
> *or take the path that sinners tread,*
> > *or sit in the seat of scoffers;*
> *but their delight is in the law of the LORD,*
> > *and on his law they meditate day and night.*
> *They are like trees*
> > *planted by streams of water,*
> *which yield their fruit in its season,*
> *and their leaves do not wither.*
>
> > > > > > > > *(Ps. 1:1–3c)*

Study the image on the next page and reread the verses from Psalm 1.

The picture is from an Egyptian tomb, drawn more than a thousand years before Christ.[2] If you study the picture closely, you will notice the living water that is beneath the earth, a primal symbol for the divine energies. The tree grows through the solar plexus of the figure bowed in prayer. The tree then extends straight upward and is filled with luxuriant foliage and plentiful fruit. It is a stunning image of someone who is keeping in touch with God, someone who is being formed by prayer into a thriving and fruitful creature of God.

According to the psalmist, meditating upon the law day and night makes the devout worshiper like a tree planted by the streams of water. It is one of the tragic legacies of much Christian preaching that the positive function of the law in keeping us in touch with God has often been neglected. Eager to speak of salvation by grace, preachers may forget that for the psalmist the law was itself a gracious gift from God, providing welcome clarity and direction for those who followed it. To meditate upon the law day and night is to make a steady diet of a good and gracious gift from God. Othmar Keel believes the Hebrew writers probably derived the image of the tree from Egypt, particularly from Egyptian wisdom literature. According to Keel, the willingness of the Hebrews to borrow from surrounding cultures suggests: "Israel did not live in isolation. It engaged in an active intellectual exchange with the world around it. Not infrequently, this posed a catastrophic threat to Israel's particularity. However, it also permitted Israel's experiences and conceptions of God to be rounded out by those of neighboring peoples."[3] Preachers help us keep in touch with God not by simplistically setting the Bible and culture against each other, but by following the example of the biblical writers who drew upon culture whenever it offered ways to strengthen the connection with the Divine.

Clogged Springs

It is revealing to hold side by side in our mind's eye the image of Michelangelo's Creator God saying, "Keep in touch," and this image of the human creature receiving the vital energies of the primal waters. The Egyptian icon and the psalmist meditating on the law day and night remind us that keeping in touch with God requires a steady discipline of prayer. It is something much more profound than merely working on next Sunday's sermon. It is a life dedicated to developing, nurturing, and strengthening a relationship to the One in whose name we speak.

When I hear preachers say that the springs have dried up, I often discover in my work with them that it would be more accurate to say: The springs have gotten clogged from neglect and lack of use. Robert Frost has a deceptively simple poem about getting the spring to run again.

> *I'm going out to clean the pasture spring;*
> *I'll only stop to rake the leaves away*
> *(And wait to watch the water clear, I may):*
> *I shan't be gone long. – You come too.*
>
> *I'm going out to fetch the little calf*
> *That's standing by the mother. It's so young*
> *It totters when she licks it with her tongue.*
> *I shan't be gone long. – You come too.*[4]

The placement of this poem in Frost's collection is significant. It is the very first poem in the poet's entire collected works. The placement of the poem suggests that cleaning out the spring is the work of imagination and creativity, represented by all the poems that follow.

The poet is not going out to dig a new well because an old one has dried up. Instead, he is going to "rake the leaves away/(And wait to watch the water clear, I may)." There is artistic and spiritual precision in these simple lines: The poet will spend his energy raking away the leaves, but the clearing of the water is not in the poet's hands. The poet will "watch the water clear." The clear water will be a gift. But the gift is not available until the labor of raking is done.

The same pattern holds for us preachers. We have to clear out the clogged spring. Our study, our prayer, our thinking, and our creating are hard labor. But when the spring starts flowing, we receive the water as a gift. Our best sermons come to us as a gift, but only after we clean out the spring.

Frost's poetic precision illumines the relationship between homiletics as method and homiletics as spirituality. The method matters. If no raking is done, the spring will never flow. But raking does not produce the water; it does not place the spring in the ground, nor replenish it with melting snow and the rains of a softer season. In learning to balance labor and receptivity in the creation of sermons, preachers are involved in a particular type of spirituality whose patterns are replicated in various ways in the lives of those to whom they preach.

Many people have the illusion that all is within human control. The prayerful disciplines of patience, of waiting upon the Lord, of opening oneself to receive realities larger than the purposeful constructions of our minds are foreign to our age. But they are not foreign to preachers who work strenuously to prepare their sermons, yet know that in the last analysis they are dependent upon gifts and powers that are far beyond their control.

The second verse of Frost's poem talks of fetching "the little calf /That's standing by the mother. It's so young/It totters when she licks it with her tongue./I shan't be gone long – You come too." Going out to clean the spring draws us toward the wonder and delight of new life. We encounter vitality, freshness, and promise—the very liveliness that marks our preaching when we are in touch with God. We often think of these as qualities that grow with practice, with reading great writers and hearing gifted preachers. All these are, in fact, ways to refine our homiletical art to the delight of our congregations and the glory of God. But I have heard preachers whose verbal art was vivid and skilled, and yet the total impact of their preaching lacked the vitality, freshness, and promise that spring from the nerve of a vital relationship with God.

"I shan't be gone long. – You come too." The final line of each stanza suggests that it will never be adequate for the poet or the preacher to clean out the spring and celebrate new life as a solitary figure. You come too—

- you the congregation
- you with your own clogged springs
- you with your particular genius for resisting the grace of God
- you with your own thirst for clear water and new life
- you who are part of a world that is panting for a refreshed spirit

You come too.

Surprised by Springs We Never Knew Before

So far I have discussed living springs and clogged springs. But now I want to name another kind of spring: those deep wells of the Spirit that we have yet to discover, springs of new life that will appear in the most unlikely places, surprising and astonishing us. "I will make the wilderness a pool of water, /and the dry land springs of water"(Isa. 41:18b). The people to whom we preach are often dry land, parched by grief or doubt or fear, often hopeless and despairing. Life is a wilderness for them, and they are desperate to renew the vitalizing energies of their existence.

Or they stay close to the springs they have, not daring to give up the water they have for fear that if they move into new territories of thought, they will find themselves lost in a barren land. I remember a time when I was afraid to move on in life because I feared my springs would dry up. I was a pastor and I had a friend, a seminary professor and former teacher of mine, who wanted me to leave the parish and return to the school to teach with him. Neither he nor the school administration could get me to budge. I had written two books and was writing a third, all based on my experience as a pastor. I feared that if I left the pastorate, my springs would dry up. I told that to my friend, and he responded with an answer that finally set me free to enter the ministry of theological education to which, I can now see, God was calling me. My friend said: "Wherever you go, you will find new springs."

I recall arriving on the seminary campus in early summer. Nearly all the students and many of the faculty were gone until fall. In the seminary apartment into which I initially moved, I sat down with the gifts that the parish had given me on my last Sunday there. The place was silent and a great hollowness filled my heart. I wanted to go back to the reliable springs I had known. Then came a knock on the door and the invitation to go to lunch with two new colleagues. We sat in the restaurant and talked and talked about new currents in biblical studies, developments in theology, how these trends in scholarship illumined my pastoral experience, and how my experience enriched and challenged assumptions and perspectives of the academy. By the time we stood, I sensed living springs welling up around and through me.

One of the preacher's tasks is to keep alive the vision of the possibility of surprising and unexpected springs. We live in a time when not just individuals, but entire societies and cultures begin to wonder if there is any way for us to redirect the brutality and violence that afflict us. Unless people believe there is the possibility of refreshing the holiest dreams of the human heart and the energy to fulfill those dreams, they will stand by whatever meager flow of life they still possess and content themselves with individual survival. The task of preaching is to affirm the possibilities that elude the range of their increasingly constricted imaginations.

Windbreath Mud Creatures

One of the chief homiletical strategies for breaking the grip of despair is to help people experience at the most basic level how the springs of the Spirit are feeding them at every moment of their existence, how God is staying in touch with them through the astonishing grace and gift of being alive. Such a statement may seem simple, even naïve, but it represents the kind of simplicity that the Shakers celebrated when they sang, "'Tis the gift to be simple...to come down where you ought to be." Preaching helps us find where we ought to be and to "come down" there, to be centered in the deep, dear core of things, to be in touch with God.

The ancient Hebrews centered themselves in holy truth, not by abstract reasoning but by their receptivity to the wonder of life. For example, they understood something as elemental as breath to be a gift from the God who breathed life into them. Michelangelo pictures Adam as a splendid athletic form, almost as much a deity as his creator. But the word *Adam* really has a much earthier, messier constellation of meanings in Hebrew. Because the word means "from the earth," at least one scholar prefers the translation "earth creature"; but since there is so much water flowing in the story, I prefer the translation "mud creature." God created *mud creature*. I am mud creature. You are mud creature. The task of preaching is to remind us of this identity, to keep us aware of how utterly incredible it is that we mud creatures should breathe in and out, in and out, in and out.

For the Hebrews this gift of breath came directly from the windbreath of God who breathes into the nostrils of mud creature. Adam then is not merely mud creature; Adam is windbreath mud creature. I am windbreath mud creature. You are windbreath mud creature. Following is the definition of what it means to know this, to "come down where we ought to be," to acknowledge the true nature of our existence, to get in touch again with God, and to find in the fact of our breath a constant, moment by moment reminder of how we are created and sustained by a power that we cannot contain nor control:

> *Each breath is borrowed air,*
> *not ours to keep and own,*

and all our breaths as one declare
what wisdom long has known:
to live is to receive
and answer back with praise
to what our minds cannot conceive:
the source of all our days.
The sea flows in our veins.
The dust of stars is spun
to form the coiled, encoded skeins
by which our cells are run:
to live is to receive
and answer back with praise
to what our minds cannot conceive:
the source of all our days.
From earth and sea and dust
arise yet greater things,
the wonders born of love and trust,
a grateful heart that sings:
to live is to receive
and answer back with praise
to what our minds cannot conceive:
the source of all our days.
And when our death draws near
and tries to dim our song,
our parting prayers will make it clear
to whom we still belong:
to live is to receive
and answer back with praise
to what our minds cannot conceive:
the source of all our days.[5]

The task of preaching is to return us to a true assessment of our actual place in creation. When preaching opens us to acknowledge our continuous dependence upon the source of all that is, we are less prone to either arrogance or despair. Aware that our very existence is grace, a gift from God, we no longer live with the illusion that we are the masters of life in control of our fate. Instead, gratitude, wonder, and worship become the defining characteristics of our life. Aware of how God's care is perpetually evident in something as simple as our breath, we live in hope that we will find new springs even when we are passing through barren and strenuous times.

Dealing with the Passion to Manage, Predict, and Control

I once heard a sound bite on the evening news that captured something of the illusory human understandings that faithful preaching dispels by pointing to our utter dependence upon God. We had been through several dry summers in Colorado, followed by winters with less than average snowfall. The prognostication was for severe drought and hazardous fires. Then in late March the mountains were hit with massive snowstorms; and there were giant accumulations of snow, bringing the promise of adequate water. There was great celebration in the newspaper. People talked about the welcome storms at parties and at work. But before the snows began to melt, the mountains were buffeted by a sirocco, an intensely arid, hot wind. The snow evaporated into the air, and never became available to us as water in our streams and reservoirs. After the winds ceased and the snow disappeared, an expert from the water management bureau said on the late night news: "It was an event that management could neither predict nor control."

Manage, predict, control: These are the words that build in the mind and heart the illusion that we are in command of life. We do, of course, have a limited capacity to manage, predict, and control portions of reality. But again and again our efforts bump up against elements that refuse to obey us: fierce dry winds assault the mountains and evaporate the snow. The truth is that there is only a finite amount of reality that we can manage, predict, and control. For we are windbreath mud creatures who keep forgetting our identity.

When the Illusion of Control Shatters

If we have succumbed to the illusion of believing we can manage, predict, and control life, we may respond to the disruptions of our existence with a desperation as fierce as that revealed in this ancient Sumerian prayer:

> *May the fury of my lord's heart be quieted toward me.*
> *May the god who is not known be quieted toward me;*
> *May the goddess who is not known be quieted toward me.*
> *May the god whom I know or do not know be quieted*
> *   toward me;*
> *May the goddess whom I know or do not know be quieted*
> *   toward me...*
> *In ignorance I have eaten that forbidden of my god;*
> *In ignorance I have set foot on that prohibited by my*
> *   goddess...*

> *When the goddess was angry with me, she made me become*
>   *ill.*
> *The god whom I know or do not know has oppressed me;*
> *The goddess whom I know or do not know has placed*
>   *suffering upon me...*[6]

This is a heartbreaking prayer. It is the cry of someone who is lost in a spiritual scramble for relief from affliction, bewildered by inscrutable possibilities. What power, what deity, what force is in control of life?

Before we dismiss this invocation as an artifact of antiquated belief, we need to consider what it reveals about the long-term purpose of preaching. Although we may not regularly speak of unknown deities, we know what it is like to be at the mercy of unseen powers. Such anguish seems to be common to the human condition. It is a state familiar to many of those who hear us preach.

Like the Sumerian, the psalmist hurls at heaven the full force of despair:

> *My God, my God, why have you forsaken me?*
>   *Why are you so far from helping me, from the words of my*
>   *groaning?...*
> *I am poured out like water,*
>   *and all my bones are out of joint;*
> *my heart is like wax;*
>   *it is melted within my breast.*

(Ps. 22:1, 14)

But notice this great difference. While the Sumerian struggles to identify the source of the affliction—the god or goddess whom I do not know—the psalmist knows exactly where to turn: "*My* God, *my* God." This is no unknown god or goddess. This is the precise, personal center of reality, the source and sovereign of creation, the deep dear core of things, the twirler of the star dust, the One who knit the macramé of the double helix molecule, the heart of our own heart who is accessible in the moment of direst need, "*My* God, *my* God." The task of preaching is to present the reality of God in ways that are so gripping people can pray with the unreserved passion of the psalmist even when they feel God has lost touch with them.

Because the One to whom the psalmist prays is a centered and integrated reality, the psalmist does not get lost in the convolutions of a diffuse and fragmented spiritual search. There are hard and bitter things to deal with, but the psalmist is liberated to express these without qualification, while the Sumerian expends spiritual energy in ways that can only magnify the anguish. Feeling at the mercy of unknown powers expands the burden of the Sumerian's suffering. The impenetrable shadow of having broken some undisclosed cosmic taboo deepens the affliction. When people are lost in such labyrinthine torments, they find it difficult if not impossible to gather together the spiritual and psychological energies that would help them get in touch with God.

But when preaching has consistently nurtured a faith strong enough to cry, "My God, my God, why have you forsaken me?" then our fragmented selves are drawn together. Faith assures us that God will not reject us for voicing our deepest hurt. The faith that empowers us to pray with the honesty and fervor of the psalmist has a salutary impact upon our whole being. Throwing the full force of our despair and hope at God opens us to realities larger than our finite, sensate selves. By freeing the expression of the heart's burden, faith makes us more accessible to the springs of the Spirit as they flow through the support of those who love us, and through the symbols and rituals that remind us that God is working in and through all who care for us.

In some shadowed corner of the Sumerian's soul, there was at least a glimpse of how wonderful such a healing faith might be. For the Sumerian prayer ends with these words:

> *May thy heart, like the heart of a real mother, be quieted*
> *toward me;*
> *Like a real mother [and] a real father may it be quieted*
> *toward me.*[7]

This irrepressible human yearning for the eternally reliable parent resonates with much that is in the Psalter and, for some of the psalmists, it is a yearning taken beyond invocation to realization:

> *I am calm and tranquil*
> *like a weaned child*
> *resting in its mother's arms:*
> *my whole being at rest.*[8]

"*My* whole being at rest" proceeds from a faith that is directed toward the center of all being, the One to whom I cry in my most desperate pain: "*My* God, *my* God, why have you forsaken me?"

This, then, is part of the most profound task of preaching: to free humans from the anxiety that drives them to the illusions of management, prediction, and control by giving witness to the source and center of all that is, by getting them once again in touch with God.

Catching the Heart Tumbling through Darkness

Or to put the whole matter another way: There is a technical term in English for people who are experts in dealing with "events that management could neither predict nor control." The technical term is *pastor* or *preacher*. A major portion of a pastor's life is spent in dealing with what management cannot predict or control. It requires skill and art to deal interpersonally with individuals and families when they go through these times; but there is also a homiletical dimension to providing a worldview, a theological understanding of human life that can bear the massive forces set off by events we cannot manage, predict, or control. When preaching keeps us in touch with God and maintains our identity as windbreath mud creatures and points us to the springs of the Spirit that sustain every moment of our life, then it creates a theological web that does not explain away tragedy and pain, but that catches the heart tumbling through the darkness before it is fragmented beyond repair.

We see John the evangelist weaving such a theological web in the way he presents the interaction between Jesus and the woman at the well (Jn. 4). When John was writing this story, his church had a sense of tumbling through the darkness because Christ had not returned, the parousia had not arrived, and Rome was still in power. Thus the story of the woman at the well is more than an interpersonal encounter with Christ. It is also a story about rediscovering the spring of faith for a community.

If ever there was someone who knew that life is filled with events we cannot manage, predict, and control, surely it was the woman at the well. There is a homiletical convention that asserts she was a woman of ill repute, but the text and the cultural practices of her day indicate this is a misreading of her situation. After she has had her conversation with Christ, many people believe in him "because of the woman's testimony" (Jn. 4:39). If she had been living a scandalous life and considered a woman of ill repute, they would not have given such credence to her testimony.

Furthermore, her succession of husbands fits into the ancient custom of a widow marrying her dead husband's brother. If this accounts for the Samaritan woman's history of five marriages, then a much more sympathetic portrait emerges. Assume for a moment that her first marriage was happy and filled with promise. One day someone comes home with the sad news that a stone tower fell on her husband and crushed him to death. The next brother in line then takes her hand in marriage. Perhaps she has worked through her grief and is ready now at last to settle into the life of which she had dreamed during the first marriage. But one day, while working in the field beneath a hot sun, her second husband suffers a heart attack and dies. Again she grieves. Again she marries. Again her husband dies. And still the pattern is not over. Again she grieves. Again she marries. Again her husband dies. Then she repeats the pattern yet another time! By now she feels cursed, as if to marry is to guarantee the death of any man who weds her. So on the sixth time, she does not marry. She does not risk another life.

I acknowledge this is speculation, but it fits much better with the obvious respect the woman enjoys in her community and with the practice of Levirate marriage than assuming she is a woman of ill repute. Also, it seems significant that Jesus does not choose to engage the woman in conversation about her marital status, but rather follows her lead when she turns the talk to theological matters (Jn. 4:19).

If, in fact, the Samaritan woman had suffered the loss of one husband after another, then the reason she came to the well at noon (Jn. 4:6b) might be not to avoid unwanted stares of condemnation but to avoid pity. For when one has been through that much tragedy, one often perceives that people are treating him or her as too fragile for normal human interaction. A mother might pull aside her child who has run up to the widow of five husbands and say, "Shush, you must not bother her. She has known great sadness." After having endured for years this well meaning but isolating behavior, the widow might have decided it was simply easier to get water when no one else was around.

Then one day the Samaritan woman meets someone who does not offer her pity, but instead assumes she still has the capacity to respond to another human being's need. "Give me a drink," says Jesus (v. 7). Imagine how those words must have sounded to the Samaritan woman. John reports she was astounded that a Jewish man would make such a public request of a Samaritan woman (v. 9). But there may have also been her astonishment at being treated without pity. Christ's simple request may have been for her like the first trickle of water from a spring long clogged. Someone asked her for a drink of water. Instead of being seen as the woman who has been through too much to ever bother with a basic human request, she was seen as fully human. And once that initial flow of vital energy was unclogged in her, she was ready to receive the living water of Christ.

The purpose of preaching is to do what Christ did for the Samaritan woman and, through her story, for the community of John. Notice how I put this; I did not speak about the purpose of a sermon but the purpose of preaching. For any particular sermon may have a particular purpose and function in the life of a congregation. But over time, the cumulative purpose of preaching is to help people keep in touch with God so that, as they spend their last borrowed breath, they may pray:

> *O Beauty so ancient and so new...*
> *you were with me,*
> *and I **was** with you...*

9

Disrupting a Ruptured World

Mary Donovan Turner

"The Spirit of the Lord is upon me,
because he has anointed me
to bring good news to the poor.
He has sent me to proclaim release to the captives
and recovery of sight to the blind,
to let the oppressed go free,
to proclaim the year of the Lord's favor."
Luke 4:18–19

With these words, Luke tells us, Jesus inaugurates his ministry. Clearly placing Jesus in the Jewish prophetic tradition, Luke revises the words of Isaiah to fit the contours of the story that is about to unfold. The purpose of Jesus' ministry? of his preaching? Here, the bringing of good news means:

- to proclaim for the captives *release* and for the blind sight
- to send forth the oppressed in *release*
- to proclaim the year of the Lord's favor[1]

In the story found in Luke 4, Jesus clearly stands in the tradition. He is in the synagogue, it is the Sabbath, and he is quoting words from Isaiah. By using these "old" words to express the "new," Jesus interprets or reinterprets the tradition for his context. He links the past with the present. He creates the possibility for something to be created and grown, a new understanding of how God is at work in the world. These words from Isaiah, spoken by Jesus, are foundational to my own understanding of the purpose of preaching.

Prophetic Roots

There are many valid and helpful places for this conversation to begin. Most of the prophetic books in the Hebrew Bible/Old Testament, the gospels, and several of the epistles use metaphors and images that try to illustrate and define for the hearer/reader the power and purpose of speaking a word from God. Who has not been inspired by the burning fire shut up in Jeremiah's bones? He was compelled to bring a harsh and definitive word to his community; he wanted them to avoid disaster. Or who has not been thrilled by the emphatic words of Isaiah to those on whom disaster had come? "Comfort, O comfort my people..." (Isa. 40:1). These and many other words from the prophets could provide a compelling birthplace for our thoughts. Each prophet brings a different field of language, different because the contexts, the needs, the unbounded desires, and the binds of their communities were radically different from one another. Thus, different interpretations of God and history emerge. Sometimes we can witness a difference in the words spoken by a single prophet, either because understandings grew over time or the context of the world radically changed, calling forth new ideas and affirmations, questions and concerns. Differences occurred, then, over time, between and within the prophets whose words have found a place in our canon.

The Ministry of Jesus through the Eyes of Luke

The quotation from Isaiah found in Luke 4 foreshadows the purposes of Jesus' ministry, his speech, his life. I am aware that preachers in many traditions, and many of my students, are not biblical preachers. And yet, it is fascinating to realize that the picture painted by Luke of the purpose of Jesus' speaking, and consequently ours, may likely be heartily embraced by them. As for me, I know nowhere else to begin. Luke 4:18–20 is, for the most part, a quotation from Isaiah 61:1–2. Language from Isaiah 58:6 has been added to verse 18: "...to let the oppressed go free." This addition repeats and emphasizes the idea of "release" as a characteristic activity of Jesus. Some bond, something oppressive must be disrupted; consequently, something is released.

Jesus' primary mission is to preach good news to the poor. The poor would include those who suffer economically; but more generally, the "poor" would include all others who live in disadvantaged conditions. Those without status or honor, those who live outside the boundaries of God's people would be included here. God has opened a way for all to belong to the family. Jesus preaches this good news by releasing the captives and by restoring sight to the blind. He does the latter in Luke by healing the blind of their physical diseases; he does this metaphorically by offering salvation. Jesus releases the oppressed; and proclaims the year of favor. If the "year of favor" is a reference to the year of the Jubilee (Lev. 25), then Jesus' ministry is about the releasing of slaves and the cancellation of debts. Normal patterns of subordination are interrupted so that, through release, life can begin again.[2]

Luke, then, has turned to Isaiah to find words that define and name Jesus' ministry. Chapters 58 and 61 call upon the servant and the community to be about this same ministry of "release." The compelling words in chapter 58 describe a community that looses the bonds of injustice, releases the oppressed, feeds the hungry, houses the homeless, covers the naked; it is a community where kin relate to kin. Isaiah describes a consequent light breaking forth and a healing that comes to the whole community. The people get a new name. It is "the repairer of the breach, /the restorer of streets to live in" (58:12b). The people are repairing the ruptured society. In chapter 61, the people also receive a new name. "They will be called oaks of righteousness, /the planting of the LORD, to display his glory" (61:3). Being righteous is to live in right relationship with neighbor and God. In both readings we experience a change, a transformation from what was to what can be. Isaiah uses the "big words of the Old Testament"–*righteousness, justice, salvation,* and *redemption.* These words have been co-opted by some religious communities; they have been privatized and diminished. But when their Hebrew meanings are recovered, we witness in them a strong sense of the "now," of community and the systemic responsibility each person holds for the other. We witness in them a strong pull toward deliverance and toward offering fullness of life to each person created by God. They call us toward change. They call us to release and be released. The call is urgent, and it is compelling.

In the extended story of Jesus and the church, related by the author of Luke–Acts, the presence of God's spirit sparks truthful and liberating speech among the most ordinary human beings. The unmistakable mark of the Spirit's presence with the people is prophetic speech. Luke–Acts demonstrates most fully the importance of the human voice in the divine realm through the story of Jesus and his followers' empowerment for proclamation. Elizabeth, who is filled with the Holy Spirit, recognizes that her cousin Mary is blessed and pours forth her witness of the fulfillment of the Lord's word. Zechariah, also filled with the Holy Spirit, speaks a prophetic word about redemption and salvation. He speaks about forgiveness and God's tender mercies. Jesus, filled with the power of the Spirit, begins to teach in the synagogues. The apostles in Acts, when filled with the Holy Spirit, proclaim the Word with boldness. (See in particular Luke 1:41, 67; 2:25, 27; 4:14, 18; Acts 4:8, 31; 7:55; 13:4–5; 18:25; 19:6.

One of the most compelling portraits of proclamation is the story of Mary, Joseph, Jesus, and Simeon in Luke 2, the lectionary reading for the first Sunday after Christmas, year B. Simeon is identified only as a "man in Jerusalem." He is righteous and devout. We can imagine, then, that he is sensitive to the needs of his neighbors and to his relationship with God. He is grounded in his tradition, faithful in his practices of ritual and the customs of his faith. He is unwavering in his loyalty and commitment. On the one hand, he represents what is old, customary, and known. But on the other hand, he speaks what is new, radical, and revolutionary. This is because, we are told, the Spirit of God hovers over all that is happening as the story unfolds. The Holy Spirit rests on Simeon and tells him that he will see the Messiah before he dies. And the Spirit guides him to the temple that day, the day Mary and Joseph appear with the infant Jesus to dedicate him to God. When Simeon sees Jesus, he praises God. He knows that God is in his presence. He knows that this is the God who authors salvation for *all* people; this is the light to the Gentiles and the glory of Israel alike. With the Spirit upon him, Simeon gives voice to a new, radically inclusive understanding of the good news. Grounded in the old, his eyes have been disciplined to see God. Windswept by the Holy Spirit, he is able to see the new. Simeon, an ordinary man in Jerusalem, bears witness to something that is radical, dynamic, and life giving. This story of Simeon leads us to an understanding of preaching that is incarnational. It is human; Simeon's own life experience gave birth to the words he spoke. But that is not the whole truth. His words and his understandings were of the Spirit, of God, both human and divine. One of these understandings without the other skews and distorts.

In Acts we witness this powerful melding of God's spirit and human voice. In the fourth chapter, Peter and John have been imprisoned for healing and carrying out their ministries of proclamation and witness. Brought before rulers, elders, and scribes, they were asked, "By what power or by what name did you do this?" (Acts 4:7b). Peter, filled with the Holy Spirit, speaks to them. The story as it unfolds bears witness to the followers of Jesus, filled with the Holy Spirit, followers who could not be silenced. "When they had prayed, the place in which they were gathered together was shaken, and they were all filled with the Holy Spirit and spoke the word of God with boldness" (Acts 4:31).

Preaching as Disruption

I wonder if any preacher hopes that when the final word of the sermon is spoken and the benediction pronounced, the lives of the individuals in the community will remain exactly the same as when the service began. I suspect not. Aren't we as preachers always hoping and/or longing that something will be different? That someone will receive a new thought, change priorities, ask a new question, be comforted, feel forgiven, or be compelled to go about their own ministries with a renewed vigor and zeal? The purpose of preaching is, as it was for the prophets and as it was for Jesus, to disrupt life so that a space can be created, a space in which the Holy Spirit can work, a space in which the community can rethink, revisit priorities, or receive. The word *disrupt* has a negative connotation, to be sure. We may think of disruptions as those things that postpone the important, that irritate, that cause prolonged waiting. Perhaps we can transform, dismantle, or subvert these associations to think about "disruption" as an interval or interlude that allows us to think about those things in our lives that are not life giving. What if we understood *disruption* as something that may irritate but, at the same time, stimulate something new? What if we understood disruption as something that challenges self-indulgence, myopic thinking, and insular understandings of faith? What myths, ideologies, beliefs, or patterns of behavior, we would then ask, need to be disrupted?

This is what Jesus perceived his own work to be. He was about disrupting the world of the poor in such a way that good news could be ushered in. He felt called to interrupt oppressions. He sought to stop them by unleashing those who were bound by the expectations of others, whose voices were silenced. He was about ushering in the realm of God.

The preacher hopes for change. This might be change that takes place suddenly. It might be incremental, sequential, a process over time. Sermons can influence us, perhaps nudge us in new and challenging directions. Perhaps those who speak and those who listen find the common patterns of their lives disrupted as they are called forth to newness; or perhaps they find their timid, wavering faith changed, disrupted, or bolstered so that they hold their ground courageously in the face of evil and suffering. The Old Testament prophets interrupted the world with a word; voice slices silence. "Hear, O heavens, and listen, O earth;/for the LORD has spoken… Ah, sinful nation" (Isa.1:2–4). "The people who walked in darkness/ have seen a great light" (Isa.9:2). "A shoot shall come out from the stump of Jesse" (11:1). "See, the LORD is riding on a swift cloud" (19:1). "Oh, rebellious children, says the LORD, who carry out a plan, but not mine" (30:1). "Draw near, O nations, to hear; O peoples, give heed!" (34:1)."Thus says the LORD…" (45:1). "Hear this, O house of Jacob" (48:1). These words from the preacher-prophet Isaiah intrude into the day-to-day lives and activities of the community.

The Protestant Heritage: Thinking Again

Protestants are the inheritors of a strong tradition of the Word. The Word historically has been the central focus of worship as communities have gathered together for healing, guidance, sustenance, and reconciliation (the classical purposes of pastoral care).[3] That inheritance—forged by the reformers in a climate of resistance and sealed in this century by neo-orthodox thinking—lays before us an understanding of Word sent from a wholly transcendent God, and spoken through biblical texts. Written word, however, is restrictive; it limits communication. Spoken word effects participation and communication. The spoken word is dialogical. It is spontaneous. Spoken words are not of the past or the future; they are of the present. There is in spoken word the potential for change, uncertainty, openness to interruption, and insecurity. Speaking is direct, personal, engaging, demanding, precarious, and vulnerable. To think about a "theology of voice" rather than a "theology of Word" for preaching, then, shifts the emphasis from an exclusive emphasis on the rigid and singular word of God to an event, a dialogue between the text and diverse voices that know of different life contexts, understandings, and experiences. In this understanding of preaching, the canon becomes not a slate of norms, but offers models of struggles and emerging visions that, through the leading of God's spirit, open us up to potential transformations. The notion of a word from God that freezes revelation at a particular point in time and within a particular text promotes disempowerment. Persons no longer take responsibility for participating in meaning making. They are passive recipients of truth. The movement from an understanding of Word to voice opens up the possibility for renewal. A metaphor of voice suggests that the Holy Spirit still speaks, gives voice to ongoing revelation in the lives of many who have been silenced.[4]

This theology of voice suggests preachers must listen carefully to the text and also to revelations that come to them through their experience in the world. The Word is contextualized through their understanding and those of their community. This is what we witness in Luke 2 as Simeon brings a word of salvation for all people. This is what we witness in Luke 4 as Jesus speaks words from the tradition, but voices them anew. A word that is divorced from its tradition, from its story, is a word that is "orphaned." It does not know its history. It does not know its past. And yet the word is not forever captive there. The speaking and listening God continues to be present, bringing new insight, challenging and interrupting a fraudulent finality of understanding. The preacher is in relationship with the Creator, the one who has given distinctive voices. Preachers are called to bring what they have, all that they have, to the task of preaching, immersing themselves imaginatively in it, naming the world and listening for the new thing that is being created. Preaching, then, is that which contextualizes the Word so that it can interrupt our living; God's spirit enables the preacher to bring it new and afresh to the community and to the world.

It is customary for homileticians to divide preaching into types, categories, or classifications. They often say preaching is prophetic (that which challenges, names oppressions, and leads us to act on behalf of the most vulnerable among us), this in contrast to preaching that is pastoral (that which comforts, assures, and affirms the community of faith). This would imply that there is a clear line of demarcation between the two; one can be easily distinguished from the other. If we use the Old Testament prophets as our examples, however, we see that the lines between the prophetic and the pastoral blur into a haze of fuzziness. The prophets bring a challenging word by naming the cruel realities of life as the people were living it; they speak words of indictment and reproach in an effort to save the community from its own self-created demise. But that is not the only word they speak. They speak startling words of hope and comfort to those who are living in the devastated condition they themselves have created by turning away from the God who loves them and yearns to be their companion. The prophets were observers. They watched. They listened. And then they named, out of their own understandings of God and the world, the realities of life. They tried to disrupt evil and call back the wayward. They also tried to disrupt despair, to soothe the wounds and pain of people living sinfully. They brought a word of grace to interrupt hopelessness, a word of reconciliation to interrupt fragmentation and isolation. The complexity of preaching is this. We are called to be both—pastoral and prophetic—but they cannot be distinguished from each other. The prophet is pastoral when the need arises. The one who is pastoral speaks the challenging word that the community needs to hear. It is complicated. At the same time, a word of challenge to the oppressor is a word of comfort to the oppressed. And, at the same time, the one who is called to speak a challenging word from God speaks from within the community. Jeremiah gives dramatic witness as a spokesperson who knows that the people do not live in life-producing ways. His words are harsh and angry. Yet, he loves the people, and his despair threatens to overwhelm him. His tears are unceasing.

Preaching and Liturgy That Contains It

It is right and helpful to think of the purpose of preaching in relation to the other parts of the liturgy in which it is found. It is undeniably true that in their togetherness, meaning is made. In some traditions, for instance, the sermon is followed by communion or eucharist. (In my own tradition, sometimes the reverse is true!) In others the sermon is followed by song. In still others it is followed by an invitation to join the church community or to make a confession of faith in Jesus Christ. In some, it is followed by communal or pastoral prayers. To consider how the sermon works toward or in concert with these is of prime importance, but this cannot be the final word. The purpose of preaching must be seen as bigger than the "container" in which it is found. Both preaching and liturgy have an "out in the world" dimension; they necessarily lead us beyond the confines of the four walls within which the community gathers.

At Pacific School of Religion, the mission statement for the M.Div. program reads as follows: "To prepare religious leaders of historic and emerging faith communities, organizations, and social movements for ministries of justice and compassion in a diverse and changing world." We are seeking to prepare leaders who, inspired by God's spirit, will find a public voice that, motivated by compassion, speaks out for justice in a fragmented and inequitable world. Our understanding of preaching, then, must be loosened from the confines of the sanctuary, and be enhanced or expanded to include the marketplace and the city gates.

The Purposes—Plural—of Preaching

In the fall semester of 2002, I asked each of my thirty-eight basic preaching students at Pacific School of Religion to write on an index card his or her one-sentence understanding of the purpose of preaching. Because PSR draws students from approximately forty different traditions/denominations/faiths I was not surprised to receive thirty-eight different responses. Here are some of them:

- to point beyond ourselves to God
- to persuade
- to participate in articulating God's alternative vision
- to give God a voice
- to illuminate truth
- to remind
- to encourage and affirm
- to make present the living Spirit
- to lead people to the love of their own wisdom
- to connect the truth of God's word to the hearer
- to mend our alienation from God
- to instruct
- to incarnate and embody the grace of God
- to escort others to live in the way and day of God
- to unwrap the gift of the gospel
- to proclaim the greatness of God
- to move people from where they are to where they can be
- to point toward the holy
- to comfort and challenge
- to invoke the empowering Word and presence of God in the hearer
- to speak for those who cannot

- to respond faithfully to God
- to offer hope
- to "speak the truth in love"
- to hold up a memory
- to be the prism through which the light of God can shine
- to create community
- to birth the movement of "Godde" in the life of the community of faith

This graphically illustrates that we cannot think of *the* purpose of preaching. We must think in the plural. In some ways, then, we must think of the many *purposes* of preaching.

Each of these responses is different. Each grows out of varied life experiences, traditions, and understandings of ministry; each fits the contours of particular communities, places, and times. Yet each in its own way speaks to a kind of interruption. In some way the sermon disrupts life as it is, in order for something new to happen. One of the synonyms for the verb *disrupt* is *to liberate*. Through the spoken word, our lives are disrupted in such a way that we are liberated or released from what is not life-giving for ourselves and for the community to find what is. Then we are empowered by God's spirit to find a bold voice in the midst of a broken, ruptured world, to speak a new and radical and revolutionary word.

10

Preaching as a Theological Venture

PAUL SCOTT WILSON

What is the purpose of preaching? What must preaching do in order to live up to its potential? What must homiletics do in the years ahead in order to strengthen the resources available for the church's preaching? My answers to these questions now are perhaps different from what they would have been when I started teaching preaching in the early 1980s. Then I gave primary emphasis to preaching as an exercise in creativity that created sparks between various poles within the sermon: the biblical text and our situation, judgment and grace, story and doctrine, pastor and prophet.[1] I still believe that creativity in preaching is vitally important, that preachers need to seek a fresh encounter with the Word and present it with simplicity and clarity in ways that communicate. What could be more important than that? Only one thing in my mind: I have come to understand that preachers can imagine the biblical scene vividly, use language efficiently, employ vivid images and metaphors, make good connections to today, tell fine stories, and harness significant tensions within the sermon, yet still leave out significant focus on God and God's action. In those earlier years I simply assumed that sermons based on the Bible would be God-centered. Thus, while creativity remains for me an essential aspect of the preacher's task, its necessary prerequisite is appropriate theological focus to ensure that the sermon is an event of God. The creativity that matters most in preaching is putting people in relationship with God, an activity for which we ultimately rely on the Holy Spirit, who alone employs our own best efforts to this effect. One of the key problems I see in the preaching landscape is the failure of sermons to focus in significant ways on God, and thus to inspire people to discipleship and lives of faith and action.

The Purpose of Preaching

During the question period at a recent public lecture on homiletics, an adult educator in the audience said, "Numerous studies indicate that the best way for people to learn is to be involved in styles of education other than lecturing. Does this suggest that the value of preaching as we know it has come to an end?" It was a good question. The woman who asked it did not find preaching to be as satisfying as small group learning. She was speaking from her own experience of preaching, and perhaps her experience is not unusual. Too often preaching falls short of the high ideal we might set for it. Many times, I have returned to her question in my mind.

Every preacher ought to be able to answer her question. As preachers, we cannot improve the quality of preaching effectively if we doubt its merits or our mandate. Clearly there is nothing wrong with the possibilities of small groups: preaching in small groups—some churches are small groups—or having small group discussion attached to preaching either during or after the worship service, depending upon the setting. This woman's question, as I understand it, ran to the deeper issue of whether preaching ought ever to be replaced by small groups. The answer we give depends upon how we understand the purpose of preaching.

Appropriately, our starting place about the purpose of preaching is with Scripture. We preach because Christ commissioned the church to do so: "Go into all the world and proclaim the good news to the whole creation" (Mk. 16:15). He sent the disciples to "proclaim the kingdom of God" (Lk. 9:2, 60). He promised to be wherever "two or three are gathered in my name" (Mt. 18:20) and to be with them "always, to the end of the age" (Mt. 28:20). He has given his followers his authority to preach such that, "whatever you bind on earth will be bound in heaven, and whatever you loose on earth will be loosed in heaven" (Mt. 16:19; 18:18). Moreover, he sent his Spirit who "will teach you at that very hour what you ought to say" (Lk. 12:12). He linked preaching with ministries of teaching and healing, and he told the seventy whom he sent that "whoever listens to you listens to me" (Lk. 10:16). Saint Paul says that "faith comes from what is heard, and what is heard comes through the word of Christ" (Rom. 10:17). This is in the tradition of Isaiah, who receives God's Word as an event of power: "so shall my word be that goes out from my mouth; /it shall not return to me empty, /but it shall accomplish that which I purpose, /and succeed in the thing for which I sent it" (Isa. 55:11).

None of this contradicts the possibility that preaching might take place in a different setting and with a different structure beyond that of traditional worship. Just as all Christ's followers are called to ministry, all are called to proclaim the good news. Still, as Ephesians 4 indicates, not all disciples have the same gifts: "The gifts he gave were that some would be apostles, some prophets, some evangelists, some pastors and teachers" (v. 11); the purpose of these various gifts is "to equip the saints for the work of ministry, for building up the body of Christ" (v. 12). Paul is not pointing to offices in an established institutional church, although in Acts and other places in the New Testament we do find permanent offices occasionally mentioned. Rather, he is speaking of the kinds of ministry Christians are to provide to one another, to ensure maturity in faith and conduct.

When Luther spoke of the priesthood of all believers, he meant that individual Christians need no priest apart from Christ to act as a mediator between themselves and God. All Christians mediate to one another God's gifts of love and grace, and all are equally responsible before God for their own faith. Luther wrote, "Although we are all equally priests, we cannot all publicly minister and teach. We ought not to do so even if we could."[2] He quoted Romans 13:1, "Let every person be subject to the governing authorities..." as a way of underlining that the authority is over earthly matters and does not extend to the authority over people's souls, which God alone has.[3] Ministers of Word and sacrament are not higher Christians; they are merely set apart through the rite of ordination by the community of faith to a life of study and discipline in order to exercise a ministry of the Word on behalf of the people: "...[T]he reason they are called pastors is that their duty is to find pasture for, or, to teach, their flock."[4] He saw preachers as defenders and upholders of the church.[5]

Calvin speaks with a similar high doctrine of preaching. He says, "For, among the many excellent gifts with which God has adorned the human race, it is a singular privilege that he deigns to consecrate to himself the mouths and tongues of men in order that his voice may resound in them."[6] In a sermon on 1 Samuel, he calls pastors and prophets "the very mouth of God."[7] Calvin cautions against getting carried away with such understandings by citing 1 Corinthians 3:7, "So neither the one who plants nor the one who waters is anything, but only God who gives the growth."

In practical terms, of course, preaching often falls short. Preachers frequently are harried during the week and may leave sermon preparation until Saturday; thus, they do not give preaching the priority it deserves. Sermons may fail to inspire, teach, or connect. Perhaps the challenge for preaching to be excellent has never been greater, for the general public today is more highly educated–hence, capable of critical thinking–than at any previous time in history. People are nonetheless not saved by the creativity of the preacher or the liveliness of the proclamation; they are saved by the Holy Spirit, who uses and inspires the preacher's efforts to be faithful to the gospel and effects change in the lives of the hearers. Anyone can stand back and criticize a sermon, yet everyone has a responsibility in preaching to listen with the expectation of encountering Christ. In other words, even as hearers are to pray for the inspiration of the preacher during the week, they are to pray for the preacher's and their own inspiration in and through the service of worship. They are to bring to the sermon an open heart and mind, actively seeking illumination, conviction, and transformation. Preaching in this sense is a partnership between God, the preacher, and the congregation in which God, of course, is the senior partner.

To my mind, there are many purposes of preaching; yet at this time for me, the primary ones are theological: Preaching is to communicate faith. It is to present the word of God in such a way that the people experience the sustenance God offers, and are thereby equipped "for the work of ministry." Such an encounter with God is an event by nature, not primarily information or abstraction; it is both informative of God's and human nature and transformative, effecting change in people's lives, and love of God and of one's neighbor.

What Must Preaching Do to Live Up to Its Potential?

We are now at a critical juncture in the life of the church. In so-called mainline denominations in particular, the ability of the church to communicate faith effectively to the next generations is in question. Of course, the future of the church is never up to humanity alone, and numbers alone cannot indicate if the church is being faithful.

We are passing through a time of great social change, and many factors outside the church affect attendance patterns–everything from the Internet to the pluralism that marks this postmodern age. The church nonetheless needs to take seriously declining membership as a serious challenge and as an opportunity for possible change. Preaching is one area that needs adjustment; for if the purpose of preaching is to communicate faith, and if it is doing that for fewer numbers, something is wrong.

Many people in recent decades have prescribed changes for preaching. Many of these changes were overdue, having to do with imagination; conversational style; orality and aurality; performance; narrative plot; the form of the text and sermon form; persuasive effect; identification; rhetorical attention to logos, pathos, and ethos; congregational thought processes; multicultural awareness; and so forth. Attention to these areas needs to be maintained, yet what looks like a declining ability to communicate faith is a theological problem and also needs a theological answer. The root of the problem lies deep in the soil of the biblical text and meanings preachers find there: Preachers often read the text and do not find God.

How ought preachers read the Bible? Is there anything they should do with the Bible that is distinctive? Only fifty years ago people commonly assumed there was only one way to read it, and every text had a single meaning. This meaning through history was referred to as the literal meaning of a text.[8] The term largely fell out of use during the last century because if texts only have one meaning– the reformers claimed it was the literal–there is no need to call it literal to distinguish it from other readings.[9]

We now know that individuals read the Bible with different needs and interests, and these lead them to find many different legitimate meanings. For instance, a teenager may look for moral guidance; a truck driver may seek security for driving on the highway; a university student may want biblical information for a course. We also know that scholarly readings produce different focuses. For instance, a New Testament professor may place special emphasis on a text's traditions or origins; a theologian may develop its doctrine; and an ethicist may explore its economic and social background. Before the fragmentation of the theological curriculum into many subjects in the decades following World War II, preaching received a much higher percentage of overall instruction time in ordination studies. My own institution required five courses per year for the B.D. degree (now the M.Div.), including one course in preaching in the first year and one in the second year, plus a year-long speech communication course in the third year. Preaching was regularly included as a focus in courses on Bible, theology, and history, which is generally not the case today. In other words, one-fifth of the program was devoted to preaching, not counting the time afforded to preaching in other classes. Integration of studies largely occurred in and through preaching. For good or ill, over the last fifty years congregational ministry has shifted to be less centered on the Word; pastors have had to become generalists in many areas; and professors are under increased pressure to specialize in their own disciplines. Not all of this has negative implications for preaching, for ministry is more complex today and some of the things formerly taught under preaching are now dealt with more properly in other disciplines. Still, on the whole, attention to preaching has diminished, and this at least coincides with and may well contribute to a period of decline in the church.

Different needs cause people to see different things when they read the Bible. When preachers now speak of the meaning of a biblical text, they do not refer to a singular meaning and generally refer to those multiple meanings that emerge on the other side of historical critical exegetical method, which is concerned primarily with what the text meant in its original setting and context. Historical criticism allows preachers to distinguish between the grammatical meaning (what the text literally says) and the historical meaning (what the text means). It provides the best way to hear the Bible in a manner roughly equivalent to how its original hearers heard it. Further, it prevents us from identifying or connecting with the past too quickly.

Exegesis is also concerned with numerous other functions around which schools of criticism have emerged and that supply additional textual meanings: for example, the human author's original words (textual criticism), the original form of the text (form criticism), the editor's handling of it (redaction criticism), the traditions it passed through (tradition criticism), and what the church meant in canonizing it as scripture for the community of faith (canonical criticism). Not all these are equally important for preaching, but it is easy to see how preachers preparing a sermon commonly have the problem of too much information and uncertainty about knowing on what best to focus.

The meanings of a text do not stop there. Historical criticism today necessarily includes literary criticism that teaches readers to look in various additional places for a text's meanings: the text's form and content separate from history (new criticism); the polar opposites in a text (structuralism); contradictions in the text (deconstruction); what the text tries to do (rhetorical criticism); what the reader does because of the text (reader response); how it engages capitalism (Marxist criticism); how it exposes patriarchy (feminist criticism) or racism (black criticism); what it says about power relationships in the culture it represents (new historicism). Textual study today also includes reference to other disciplines like geography, comparative religion, sociology, anthropology, archeology, and psychology.

One result of these multiplying and often competing meanings is the threat to the ability of the Bible to function as the norm for faith and doctrine. Who is to say what meanings are most important? Many biblical scholars are no longer confident in speaking about the Bible as the word of God. When faced with a perceived conflict between a text's human and divine dimensions, biblical scholars increasingly allow the human to win out. History has gradually taken over the interpretation of texts, often to the exclusion of theological meanings. As theologians Carl E. Bratten and Robert W. Jenson say, "The methods of critical reason have tended to take over the entire operation of biblical interpretation, marginalizing the faith of the church and dissolving the unity of the Bible as a whole into a multiplicity of unrelated fragments."[10] Faith is commonly seen as something that can jeopardize a fair reading of the text.

We return now to our earlier question about whether there is a distinctive way preachers approach the Bible. Preachers need to use all means available to help them to understand the text, simply because texts are so pregnant with meaning. When they come to preparing a sermon, however, they need to recover the Bible not as the academy's book but as the church's book. The church studies the Bible as sacred scripture, as revelation, listening for the word of God; and preachers cannot preach effectively until that encounter has taken place.

The key meanings of a text for preaching are thus discerned by asking not only historical and literary questions of the text but theological questions as well. The purpose of theological questions is to focus on God and God's action in the past and present, and the promise of that action in the future. We can ask, "Who is God (in one of the Persons of the Trinity) in this text?" or "What is God's nature in this text?" or "What is God doing in this text?" If God is not mentioned, we might ask, "What is God doing behind this text in the larger historical picture?" or, "Why was this text identified as God's Word and preserved as such?" or even, "What does this text call us rightly to believe?" There are various ways in which we can get to the heart of the text as scripture, and there is no need to review more options here in order to highlight their importance.[11] I am saying that preachers need theological criticism, in addition to historical criticism, to develop the text as scripture. They need to find the God meanings or what we may call the God sense or senses of a text in order to preach it. When theological questions are not asked, and when the text is not engaged from the perspective of faith as the church's book, the text's capacity to speak to faith is removed from it. Most preachers omit from their sermons significant discussion of God and focus instead on human action.[12] This is one of the key reasons many sermons fail in their chief purpose, which is to communicate faith. By focusing on history or on human action alone, God's role in human life is obscured and God's resources for human change are ignored.

We have been discussing what preaching must do in order to live up to its potential. In addition to recovering the Bible as scripture, I hope that preachers will recover preaching as a theological exercise. Theology is discussion about God and God's relationship to humanity and all creation. Understanding preaching as a theological task can provide a safeguard against sermons becoming excessively focused on one pericope or text to the exclusion of how that text relates to the larger gospel message or teachings of scripture. Our ancestors understood better than we do that when we preach, we preach from one text but not only one text; we preach the Bible. In other words, the text upon which we focus is already in dialogue with other biblical texts and teachings; and part of our role as preachers is to lift up this larger Christian story.

A further implication of preaching as theology is sermon structure. In previous eras, when preachers were encouraged to preach the entire Bible and suffered less from the constraints of time on the worship service, they had forty to sixty minutes to preach and plenty of opportunity to explore both the human and divine sides of theological relationship. How they proceeded was perhaps less of an issue than it is today. Now, with sermons often needing to be compressed below fifteen or twenty minutes, preachers may leave no time to develop a sense of God within the sermon. To avoid this,

I speak of the sermon as four Pages (or quarters) with the first half devoted to trouble (first in the text and then in our world, Pages One and Two), and the second half devoted to grace (first in the text and then in our world, Pages Three and Four). Trouble need not be conceived as only the scolding sort that is difficult to listen to; it can also be the descriptive sort that talks about life as it is in a fallen creation, that needs the power and remedy God alone can offer. And grace need not be limited to forgiveness; it also has to do with God's intervention in human affairs to bring forth God's will. Keeping trouble and grace distinct in the sermon is somewhat artificial, for the word that condemns can also be the word that saves. The purpose of keeping them separate in the sermon, however, is for each to be experienced in turn; otherwise, the distinctive flavor of the Word is lost in a soup of blended flavors. Trouble makes no demand and grace seems trivial. That sermons should end in grace upholds the character of the Christian faith as hope that prevails even in the midst of trouble.

Any sermon that focuses on God focuses on either trouble or grace, whether or not the preacher is aware of this. Trouble puts the burden on people to get their lives right; grace puts the burden on God in Christ. Whenever we preach only trouble or grace, we are in danger of misrepresenting the Word. These two sides of the Word are two sides, two expressions of God's love. They represent the tension between the exodus and the promised land, or expulsion from Eden and the return to the New Jerusalem, or between the cross and resurrection. The one indicates the end of our own attempts to save ourselves; the other indicates the sufficiency of God's saving grace each day unto itself. God's Word is a two-sided coin, and both demands change and empower it.

On a practical level, when a sermon is preached without both trouble and grace, this is not because a text fails to yield either, for preachers can learn to read texts for both. Rather, it is an expression of the preacher's lack of experience in dealing with such matters. Preachers can begin their sermons by identifying a theme sentence of the sermon that will be the subject of Page Three. They can find a trouble statement to be the subject of Page One by looking at something of the underside of the theme sentence, essentially asking, "What was the trouble that was the occasion for God to act in this way?" Such linking can help ensure that the first and second halves will result in one unified sermon, not two.

What Homiletics Must Do to Strengthen Preaching

What must homiletics do in the coming years in order to strengthen the resources available for the church's preaching? We have been conceiving of preaching as bringing people to faith through public proclamation of the Word. Of course, there are many other definitions of preaching and its purpose. Homiletics is reflection on the art of preaching; thus, it is as wide ranging in subject and expression as the possible definitions of preaching. So much of what homiletics does is helpful; and thus on one hand, homiletics must continue to develop its strengths. Four recent books are examples of what it does best.

Stephen Farris's *Preaching That Matters: The Bible and Our Lives* might be the book of choice for those who want practical help with biblical exegesis that draws on both historical and literary criticism. His principle of analogy assists preachers in determining the nature of the listeners' encounters with the Word. Analogy establishes a point of similarity between two things and moves from the better known to the lesser known, or in this case from what God is saying in the Bible to what God is saying on "this side" of the analogy. Part of what makes for a strong homiletical offering is the author's willingness to work with practical matters that will benefit preachers and improve sermons. Farris has a section on "Finding the Analogies" that moves through several steps that preachers can easily follow; he demonstrates that establishing the right analogy can move a sermon well on its way toward completion.[13]

David L. Bartlett's *Between the Bible and the Church: New Methods for Biblical Preaching* is a strong theoretical offering. He argues for continued reliance upon historical criticism as the essential foundation for biblical study and the means to determine what the text says, what it meant, and what it means. Historical criticism provides a basis for conversing with various contemporary critical approaches to the Bible. He provides an excellent and brief overview of new criticism, narrative criticism, reader-response, deconstruction, and new historicism. He is passionate that preaching should make a difference in peoples' lives: "We are so scared of allegorizing and psychologizing that we may be afraid of mattering...We preach as if we were going to be graded by our seminary Bible professors, not as if we wanted to change the lives of our people."[14]

Nancy Lammers Gross has written a fine study, *If You Cannot Preach Like Paul...* in which she suggests that preachers ought to "Do what Paul did; don't just say what Paul said."[15] With Paul, preachers are "bringing the new reality of Christ's lordship into an engagement with the context in which our hearers live, in order to point the way to new life in Christ."[16] Instead of thinking of Paul's letters as answers, we are to think of them as conversations with particular situations propelled by his urgent sense of the lordship of Jesus.[17] Thus, we are imaginatively to place ourselves in the same kind of situation with his same sense of urgency, and discover what we are led to say in the process of dynamic interchange with various textual conversation partners. I value not just Gross's attempt to be more faithful to Paul, but also her readiness to query traditional hermeneutical and homiletical models like the kernel of truth and the exegesis/bridge/application models. Homiletics must pay attention to how preachers may both understand and control the homiletical actions they engage.

Finally, Haddon W. Robinson has brought out a second edition of his *Preaching Biblically: The Development and Delivery of Expository Messages.*[18] This is the most widely used homiletics book of the last century (more than two hundred thousand copies in print), and this revised edition is a masterpiece of clarity and homiletical simplicity. Robinson is in the evangelical tradition and upholds expository preaching, blending the best of it with new understandings of inductive and other approaches. In this edition he is sensitive to many issues, including ordination of women.

These are only four examples that help to indicate homiletics is at its best when it engages both theory and practice with a view to help preachers: (a) to understand what they do, and (b) to compose better sermons with greater efficiency. On one hand, then, homiletics needs to continue to develop its strengths and not get sidetracked from its purpose, which I understand to be the pastoral task of improving preaching. Beyond this, I have three suggestions. First, homiletics generally needs to be more academic, by which I do not mean more abstract—it simply needs to be more responsible about engaging or building upon what has already been said by others. So many people who write about preaching find an apple that has fallen from the homiletical tree, and write about it as though this is the first apple that has fallen and no one has commented on the phenomenon before. One could say, looking at the list of publications on preaching, that homiletics may be too much influenced by fads, too ready to divide into camps, and too little attentive to whether any new theory it proposes actually works in producing better sermons. Homiletical theory is best when it is in obvious dialogue with and tested by sermon practice.

A second suggestion is that homiletics pays more attention to what makes an excellent sermon. This issue came into focus recently for me at an annual meeting of the Academy of Homiletics[19] when Ron Allen and I made a presentation on teaching introductory preaching courses: Are we best to teach as many approaches as possible, or choose one approach to provide some solid foundations? We had this discussion because we teach basic homiletics differently. Ron provides several methods, and I teach essentially one approach that can be adapted to many forms. Neither of us knows which approach is best. Neither of us has done research to determine the best way to teach homiletics. Neither of us has been able to determine an effective tool to do so. We might interview and test students on their homiletical competence and knowledge as they depart from seminary, and again at five and ten years out. Still, how would we test homiletical competence? How would we identify the best sermons? Is it by faithfulness to the biblical text? Engaging one's theological tradition? Preaching to felt needs in the congregation? Bringing contemporary experience effectively before the Word? Dynamic delivery? Prayerful personal reflection? Active social concern? All of these can be important. What is the role of congregational participation in such an assessment? How could we avoid assessing personalities? There seem to be too many homiletical variables to make a meaningful study, yet as teachers of preaching we all make these assessments on an individual basis whenever we grade or otherwise respond to a sermon.

Maybe collectively those of us who are homileticians are part of the problem: We may take ourselves too seriously. Given the small place of homiletics in most theological curricula, just how much credit for good preaching can a homiletician assume? In these postmodern times, moreover, could we ever agree even on basic teaching standards? Many issues seem to prevent meaningful research in homiletical instruction. Still, I cannot help but lament our collective failure in our discipline to keep evaluation as a topic of ongoing concern and dialogue in our publications. Our failure may be self-serving. As long as we do not identify basic standards and do not develop common language with which to articulate homiletical concerns, we have little guidance to offer others about teaching and receive little encouragement to change. How would we even assess an improvement?

Ron and I both like his multiple approaches: invite students to a "smorgasbord" with a wide array of sermon forms and approaches.[20]

Students presumably taste each offering and may help themselves to what they like. They may even develop a hybrid style of their own, as some of our colleagues encourage. Seminaries typically serve various denominational and cultural constituencies where this openness can be particularly helpful. When students go from this smorgasbord to their own congregations, they have their lunchboxes packed with a variety of sermon sandwich models that will allow for weekly variety. This is how Ron speaks of his own approach to teaching:

> ...I try to help students identify and think critically about several different approaches to the sermon. I hope that two things happen in the introductory course. (a) I want students to begin to find ways of expressing their witness to the gospel through preaching in their own voices. Few students complete this task in the introductory course, or even in seminary....The basic course tries to provide resources from the Bible, church history, theology, and other places to help them bring their own preaching voices to expression. (b) I want students to recognize the importance of being able to transcend their own preferences in preaching when the gospel witness calls for it.[21]

By contrast, I mainly save instruction in the varieties of sermons for advanced classes. By doing so, I risk that students who take only one preaching class may get only one approach. I nonetheless take the risk for several reasons. First, if introductory students learn several models, they may learn no method well and may conclude that anything goes, as it does in some pulpits. Whenever I have been taught an art, I have first been taught basic principles and simple tasks. I learned the piano by practicing scales and playing gradually more difficult pieces, in other words, by observing a *discipline* (a word I still resist and value). Further, to my mind not all homiletical methods assist excellent preaching. A student may master a particular form and still have a poor sermon because it is biblically or theologically weak.

Perhaps the differences between these approaches to teaching do not need to be resolved, since there are obvious advantages to each. More discussion of excellence in sermons might lead, however, to improved teaching methods, whatever route one takes.

Second, another related area for homiletical improvement is in the development of homiletical guidelines and rules. Part of the homiletical task is to identify homiletical strategies that arise from actual sermons, both present day and historical. Theses rules correspond to something like a deep grammar in sermon language and contribute to effective sermon composition. Rules of classical rhetoric were devised in ancient Greece by observing excellent oral discourse, and guidelines for homiletics similarly can be devised from the practice of excellent preachers. Homiletical rules are like rules of rhetoric or rules of grammar: In their observance they facilitate effective communication. Here I think, for instance, of Tom Long's distinction between focus statement and function statement;[22] Henry Mitchell's controlling idea and behavioral purpose;[23] David Buttrick's guidelines for homiletical "moves";[24] and my own discussion of concerns of the text and concerns of the sermon.[25] These guidelines can be set aside very effectively at times. They may be less universal than some grammatical rules, geared as they are to particular cultures and specific theological understandings about the nature of a sermon and God's Word. At their best, however, they allow potential difficulties to be identified before precious time is wasted on something that is unlikely to work well. If one violates good rules too often, one increases the chances of miscommunication.

Numerous issues in homiletics remain in need of exploration and development. For example, as teachers we do not know all there is to know about the relationship of grace to sermon language and hermeneutics. Students can be taught how to discern grace and trouble in nearly any text, since they are two ways of considering the same Word. What does this say about our common way of reading biblical texts when we may not notice either? Or from the other side, if we do not notice either, what does this say about reading the text for trouble and grace? Is the possible movement to the cross and resurrection in a sermon to be understood as a legitimate extension of the text to its context in the gospel message, or is it to be understood as an application of the text, of a similar sort to the application we make of texts to today? To use the language of Sandra Schneiders, is it a matter of accommodating the text?

> The biblical text has always been used in a so-called accommodated sense in the homiletic and pastoral tradition of the Church, and often in its theological tradition. Accommodation refers to the use of a text independently of its *con*-text. Thus, by definition, accommodated meaning is not textual meaning.... It would seem that there are two

criteria that must be applied in judging the validity of an accommodated interpretation of a text. The first is whether the text *can legitimately be removed* from its original context without distorting its sense or destroying its reference; the second is whether the new context into which it is inserted is *susceptible of receiving* it and being illuminated by it.[26]

In homiletics, are we to understand the text of a sermon in the same way that a biblical scholar defines text as a unit of scripture, or is the text of a sermon more appropriately considered to be that unit *and* its connections to the entire gospel message? Are we right to distinguish between textual and accommodated meaning, as Schneiders suggests, given that the text only begins to function as scripture when it intersects with our lives? Where might textual meaning end? These questions may sound very theoretical, but they are the kinds of questions homiletics needs to address because how we answer them will have practical implication for how we prepare sermons.

A third and final area much in need of development is the subject of ethics and its role in sermons. How are preachers best to encourage the ethical life that leads from the gospel, an excitement to obedience that marks Calvin's third use of the law? Ethical life should be a natural result of receipt of the gospel message. Effective sermons generally imply an action that the congregation might undertake in the coming week (akin to Long's function statement and Mitchell's behavioral purpose). If this is our practice, we effectively employ something of the banished moral sense of scripture used by the ancient church each time we preach, for we assume that every text has something to say about how we live our lives.

At the same time we know that sermons in previous ages, even from people like John Wesley who were social activists, contain surprisingly little comment on these subjects; it is as though social ministry was lived, not preached, and it was so present in people's thoughts and weekly lives that it did not need to be discussed in the sermon. On the other hand, much preaching in all churches might loosely be considered as ethical, though more accurately it is moralistic: The gospel message becomes do's and don'ts that have an anthropocentric flavor. From a preaching perspective, substantial treatment of ethics and substantial focus on grace and faith almost seem to be at odds. Some reasons for this are clear. It takes a good deal of sermon time to develop effectively the trouble from a biblical text for today, and it takes as long in a sermon to develop a dependence upon God. Ethical analysis demands more sermon time than many preachers have, and more carefully nuanced thought than many congregations want or are able to follow. Major discussion of an ethical issue in a biblical sermon can easily be heard as trouble and has the potential to divide the congregation. Sermons are oral exercises and ought not to sound like essays and lectures, yet ethical analysis easily becomes either. I offer ethics simply as one area where homiletics is lacking.

Perhaps every age must learn to preach all over again. What one age knows instinctively, another must strain to understand or put into practice. I once hoped to have answers to most of my homiletical questions, but I find new ones that demand new solutions keep cropping up. As homileticians and preachers, we may not have the answers; but by keeping preaching and homiletics in close dialogue as partners, we may have better answers than we had. If they do not last to the next age, they may at least help the preaching of this age to be what God wants it to be.

Notes

Chapter 1: Preaching as Mutual Critical Correlation through Conversation

[1]For nuances in the contemporary preaching community's growing understanding of preaching as conversation, the preeminent works are now: John S. McClure, *Other-wise Preaching: A Postmodern Ethic for Homiletics* (St. Louis: Chalice Press, 2000), esp. 59–62, 101–13; and Lucy Atkinson Rose, *Sharing the Word: Preaching in the Roundtable Church* (Louisville: Westminster John Knox Press, 1997). A more fully developed form of my views can be found in Ronald J. Allen, *Interpreting the Gospel: An Introduction to Preaching* (St. Louis: Chalice Press, 1998); cf. Reuel Howe, *Partners in Preaching* (New York: Seabury Press, 1967); Clark M. Williamson and Ronald J. Allen, *The Teaching Minister* (Louisville: Westminster/John Knox Press, 1991), 94–96; John S. McClure, *The Four Codes of Preaching: Rhetorical Strategies* (Philadelphia: Fortress Press, 1991), 68–71; William E. Dorman and Ronald J. Allen, "Preaching as Hospitality," *Quarterly Review* 14, no. 3 (1994): 295–310; John S. McClure, *The Roundtable Pulpit: Where Leadership and Preaching Meet* (Nashville: Abingdon Press, 1995); Lucy Atkinson Rose, "Conversational Preaching," *Journal for Preachers* 14, no. 1 (1995): 26–30; John S. McClure, "Conversation and Proclamation: Several Resources and Issues," *Homiletic* 22, no. 1 (1997): 1–13; Ronald J. Allen, "Why Preach from Passages in the Bible?" in *Preaching as a Theological Task: World, Gospel, Scripture*, ed. Thomas G. Long and Edward Farley (Louisville: Westminster John Knox Press, 1996), 180–82; Lucy Hind Hogan, "*Homiletos*: The Never Ending Conversation," *Homiletic* 21, no. 2 (1996): 1–10; Clark M. Williamson and Ronald J. Allen, *Adventures of the Spirit: A Guide to Worship from the Perspective of Process Theology* (Lanham, Md.: University Press of America, 1997), 113–58; Eugene L. Lowry, *The Sermon: Dancing the Edge of Mystery* (Nashville: Abingdon Press, 1997); and Ronald J. Allen, *Preaching Is Believing: The Sermon as Theological Reflection* (Louisville: Westminster John Knox Press, 2002), 49–62. I am particularly indebted to the work of John S. McClure.

[2]Howe, *Partners in Preaching*, 47.

[3]Hans-Georg Gadamer, *Truth and Method*, trans. Garrett Barden and John Cumming (New York: Crossroad, 1982), 347.

[4]Ibid., 330.

[5]Ronald J. Allen, "Preaching and the Other," *Worship* 76 (2002), 211–24.

[6]Gadamer, *Truth and Method*, 347.

[7]David Tracy, *Plurality and Ambiguity: Hermeneutics, Religion and Hope* (San Francisco: Harper and Row, 1987), 18.

[8]Ibid., 19.

[9]Clark M. Williamson, *A Guest in the House of Israel: Post-Holocaust Church Theology* (Louisville: Westminster/John Knox Press, 1993), 13; cf. id., *Way of Blessing, Way of Life: A Christian Theology* (St. Louis: Chalice Press, 1999), esp. 2–12.

[10]Justo and Catherine González, *The Liberating Pulpit* (Nashville: Abingdon Press, 1994), 47.

[11]See Allen, "Why Preach from Passages in the Bible?"

[12]E.g., Allen, *Interpreting the Gospel*, 111–12; id., *Preaching Luke–Acts*. Preaching Classic Texts (St. Louis: Chalice Press, 2000).

[13]Williamson, *Way of Blessing, Way of Life*, 32–37.

[14]For sustained reflection on the role of systematic theology and preaching, see Allen, *Preaching Is Believing*.

[15]McClure, *The Roundtable Pulpit*.

[16]Paul Tillich, *Systematic Theology: Three Volumes in One* (Chicago: University of Chicago Press, 1967), 1:30–31, 62–66; 2:13–16.

[17]Paul Tillich, "You Are Accepted," in his *The Shaking of the Foundations* (New York: Charles Scribner's Sons, 1948), 153–63.

[18]E.g., David Tracy, *Blessed Rage for Order: The New Pluralism in Theology* (Minneapolis: The Winston Seabury Press, 1975), 45–47, 79–81; id., *The Analogical Imagination: Christian*

Theology and the Culture of Pluralism (New York: Crossroad, 1981), 371–72, 405–11, 421–23; id., "Theological Method" in Peter C. Hodgson and Robert H. King, eds., *Christian Theology: An Introduction to Its Traditions and Tasks,* revised and enlarged (Philadelphia: Fortress Press, 1985), 35–60, esp. 52–59; id., "Hermeneutical Reflections in the New Paradigm," in *Paradigm Change in Theology,* ed. Hans Küng and David Tracy, trans. Margaret Kohl (Edinburgh: T & T Clark, 1989), 334–62. While not operating under the rubric of mutual critical correlation, a similar spirit animates David Buttrick, *A Captive Voice: The Liberation of Preaching* (Louisville: Westminster John Knox Press, 1994), 110–12, as well as Edward Farley, "Preaching the Bible and Preaching the Gospel," *Theology Today* 51 (1994), 90–103; id., "Toward a New Paradigm for Preaching," in *Preaching as a Theological Task: World, Gospel, Scripture,* ed., Thomas G. Long and Edward Farley (Louisville: Westminster/John Knox Press, 1996), 176–88.

[19]Readers hear in the background Paul Ricoeur's "hermeneutic of suspicion," e.g., his *Freud and Philosophy: An Essay in Interpretation,* trans. Denis Savage (New Haven; Yale University Press, 1970). Similar concerns are expressed in contemporary ideology criticism, e.g., Beverly J. Stratten, "Ideology," in *Handbook of Postmodern Biblical Interpretation,* ed. A. K. M. Adam (St. Louis: Chalice Press, 2000), 120–27; G. A. Yee, "Ideological Criticism," in *Dictionary of Biblical Interpretation,* ed. John H. Hayes (Nashville: Abingdon Press, 1999), vol. 1, 534–37; Robert P. Carroll, "Ideology," in *A Dictionary of Biblical Interpretation,* ed. R. J. Coggins and J. L. Houlden (London: SCM Press; and Philadelphia: Trinity Press International, 1990), 309–11.

[20]Williamson, *Way of Blessing, Way of Life,* 29–32.

[21]For the derivation of these criteria, see Williamson and Allen, *The Teaching Minister,* 75–82; id., *A Credible and Timely Word: Process Theology and Preaching* (St. Louis: Chalice Press, 1991), 71–90; Williamson, *Way of Blessing, Way of Life,* 29–32.

[22]Clark M. Williamson, "Preaching the Gospel: Some Theological Reflections," *Encounter* 49 (1988): 191–92.

[23]Ibid., 194.

[24]Ibid.

[25]For differences in patterns of believability in the premodern, modern, and postmodern worlds, see Ronald J. Allen, Scott Black Johnston, and Barbara Shires Blaisdell in *Theology for Preaching: Authority, Truth, and Knowledge of God in a Postmodern Ethos* (Nashville: Abingdon Press, 1997).

[26]David Kelsey, *The Uses of Scripture in Recent Theology* (Philadelphia: Fortress Press, 1975), 170–74.

[27]Clark M. Williamson and Ronald J. Allen, *The Teaching Minister,* 78.

[28]Williamson, "Preaching the Easter Faith," *Encounter* 37 (1976): 41–52.

[29]I detail a twenty-seven step model for this congregation in *Interpreting the Gospel,* 97–176. While the reader may initially fear that these twenty-seven steps are too burdensome for weekly use, my students report that many of them quickly become almost second nature.

[30]The preacher can often find help in these early phases in the preaching conversation from the relatively new discipline of congregational studies, e.g., Thomas Edward Frank, *The Soul of the Congregation: An Invitation to Congregational Reflection* (Nashville: Abingdon Press, 2000), esp. 163ff.; Nora Tubbs Tisdale, *Preaching as Local Theology and Folk Art* from Fortress Resources for Preaching (Minneapolis: Fortress Press, 1997), 64–77; Nancy T. Ammerman, Jackson W. Carroll, Carol S. Dudley, William McKinney, *Handbook for Congregational Studies,* rev. ed. (Nashville: Abingdon Press, 1998); Allison Stokes and David Roozen, "The Unfolding Story of Congregational Studies" in *Carriers of Faith: Lessons from Congregational Studies* (Louisville: Westminster/John Knox Press, 1991), 183–92.

[31]See the literature in n. 21.

[32]See John S. McClure, *The Roundtable Pulpit: Where Leadership and Preaching Meet* (Nashville: Abingdon Press, 1995) and Lucy Atkinson Rose, *Sharing the Word: Preaching in the Roundtable Church* (Louisville: Westminster John Knox Press, 1997).

[33]Tracy, *Plurality and Ambiguity,* 22–23.

[34]Ronald J. Allen, ed., *Patterns of Preaching: A Sermon Sampler* (St. Louis: Chalice Press, 1998); cf. Mark Barger Elliott, *Creative Styles of Preaching* (Louisville: Westminster John Knox Press, 2000) which presents nine categories of preaching; and Thomas G. Long and Cornelius Plantinga, Jr., *A Chorus of Witnesses: Model Sermons for Today's Preacher* (Grand Rapids: Eerdmans, 1994) which organizes material under four rubrics—sources, aims, forms, and occasions.

[35]For a more complete description, see *Patterns of Preaching,* 117–23.

[36]Cf. *Patterns of Preaching,* 98–103.

[37]Fred B. Craddock, *As One Without Authority*, rev. ed. (St. Louis: Chalice Press, 2001), 98–101.

[38]Cf. *Patterns of Preaching*, 57–63. I discuss the uses of experience and reason in ways that Wesley did not intend by taking experience much more broadly, and by associating reason and worldview.

[39]Russell L. Dicks, "The Sacrament of Conversation," *Pastoral Psychology* 2 (May 1951): 17–21.

Chapter 2: Resisting the Powers

[1]Portions of this article are taken from Charles L. Campbell, *The Word before the Powers: An Ethic of Preaching* (Louisville: Westminster John Knox Press), 2002. Used by permission.

[2]WA, 25, 253. Thanks to Justo González and Judi Holley for translating the Latin. See also Heiko Oberman, "The Preaching of the Word in the Reformation," *Harvard Divinity Bulletin* 25, no. 1 (Oct. 1960): 9.

[3]William Stringfellow, *An Ethic for Christians and Other Aliens in a Strange Land* (Waco, Tex.: Word Books, 1973; 3d paperback ed., 1979), 29–30.

[4]Walter Wink, *Unmasking the Powers: The Invisible Forces That Determine Human Existence* (Philadelphia: Fortress Press, 1986), 59. For Wink's fuller treatment of the demonic in *Unmasking the Powers*, see 41–68.

[5]Stringfellow, *An Ethic for Christians*, 143.

[6]Ibid., 144–45.

[7]Ched Myers, *Binding the Strong Man: A Political Reading of Mark's Story of Jesus* (Maryknoll, N.Y.: Orbis Books, 1988), 141–42.

[8]Ibid.

[9]Ibid., 194.

[10]As Walter Wink has persuasively argued, the actions in Matthew 5:38–42 ("turning the other cheek," "giving the cloak also," and "going the second mile") are not acts of passivity, but acts of nonviolent resistance to the powers of domination. See Walter Wink, *Engaging the Powers: Discernment and Resistance in a World of Domination* (Minneapolis: Fortress Press, 1992), 175–89.

[11]See Dietrich Bonhoeffer, *The Cost of Discipleship*, rev. ed., trans. R. H. Fuller (New York: Macmillan, 1959).

[12]In this brief article, I am not able to delineate specific practices. The practices on which preachers focus will depend on the text used for the sermon and the congregation in which the sermon is preached. The practices will be those that resist control, domination, and violence.

[13]Nancy Duff, "The Significance of Pauline Apocalyptic for Theological Ethics," in *Apocalyptic and the New Testament: Essays in Honor of J. Louis Martyn*, eds. Joel Marcus and Marion L. Soards, *Journal for the Study of the New Testament, Supplement Series,* 24 (Sheffield: JSOT Press, 1989), 290–91. As Duff notes, while confession of guilt is essential for true repentance, it is not a helpful motivation to action.

[14]Michael Warren, *At This Time, in This Place: The Spirit Embodied in the Local Assembly* (Harrisburg, Pa.: Trinity Press International, 1999), 69.

[15]Ibid., 56.

[16]Ibid., 22.

[17]Duff, "Pauline Apocalyptic," 286–87.

[18]David A. DeSilva, *Perseverance in Gratitude: A Socio-Rhetorical Commentary on the Epistle "to the Hebrews"* (Grand Rapids: Eerdmans, 2000), 355.

[19]Many commentators refer to Hebrews as a "sermon" and the writer as a "preacher." See, for example, DeSilva, *Perseverance in Gratitude,* and Thomas G. Long, *Hebrews* (Louisville: Westminster John Knox Press, 1997).

Chapter 3: Seeing Jesus

[1]Lucy Atkinson Rose, *Sharing the Word: Preaching in the Roundtable Church* (Louisville: Westminster John Knox Press, 1997).

[2]Lucy A. Rose, "Conversational Preaching: A Proposal," a paper presented to the Academy of Homiletics, Dec. 1995, 34.

[3]Ibid.

[4]Ibid.

[5]Rose, *Sharing the Word,* 60.

[6]Rose, "Conversational Preaching," 34.

[7]Rose, *Sharing the Word,* 98.

[8]Richard Lischer, *A Theology of Preaching* (Nashville: Abingdon Press, 1981), 73.

[9]See, for example, Dorothy Sayers, *The Mind of the Maker* (San Francisco: Harper & Row, 1941).

[10]This definition of *incarnation* represents a combination of the views of Alla Bozarth-Campbell, *The Word's Body: An Incarnational Aesthetic of Interpretation* (Tuscaloosa, Ala.: University of Alabama Press, 1979) and Louise Rosenblatt, *The Reader, The Text, The Poem: The Transactional Theory of the Literary Work* (Carbondale, Ill.: Southern Illinois University Press, 1994).

[11]Charles L. Bartow, *God's Human Speech: A Practical Theology of Proclamation* (Grand Rapids: Eerdmans, 1997), 26.

[12]Eugen Rosenstock-Huessy, *Speech and Reality* (Norwich: Argo Books, 1970), 120.

[13]Gustav Niebuhr, "Religion Goes to Market to Expand Congregations," *The New York Times,* 18 April 1995.

[14]Phillips Brooks, *Lectures on Preaching* (Grand Rapids: Baker Book House, 1969), 8.

[15]Ibid.

[16]Alla Bozarth-Campbell, *The Word's Body,* 52.

[17]P. T. Forsyth, *Positive Preaching and the Modern Mind* (Grand Rapids: Baker Books House, 1980), 349.

Chapter 4: The Action Potential of Preaching

[1] "Neurophysiology," *Microsoft® Encarta® Encyclopedia 99* (Microsoft Corporation, 1993–1998). All rights reserved.

[2]"Action Potential," *Encarta®.*

[3]"Neurophysiology," *Encarta®.*

[4]James Abbington, *Let Mount Zion Rejoice: Music in the African American Church* (Valley Forge, Pa.: Judson Press, 2001), 111.

[5]Teresa Fry Brown, "An African American Woman's Perspective" in *Preaching Justice: Ethnic and Cultural Perspective,* ed. Christine M. Smith (Cleveland: United Church Press, 1998), 49.

[6]See Teresa Fry Brown, *God Don't Like Ugly: African American Women Handing on Spiritual Value* (Nashville: Abingdon Press, 2000) for an extensive discussion on moral discourse, spiritual values.

[7]S. N. Eisenstadt, "Social Change, Differentiation, and Evolution" in *The American Sociological Review* 29, no. 3 (1964): 375–86.

[8]James Harris, *Preaching Liberation* (Minneapolis: Fortress Press, 1995), 38.

[9]Micah 6:6–8, Matthew 25:13, Matthew 22:34–40 in *Bible Test: The New Revised Standard Version Bible* (Division of Christian Education of the National Council of Churches in the United States of America, 1989).

Chapter 5: Alpha, Omega, and Everything in Between

[1]An earlier version of this essay was presented at the annual meeting of the Academy of Homiletics, Boston, Massachusetts, December, 2002. I am grateful to my colleagues for their help, critiques, and suggestions.

[2]Read through the book of Jeremiah, and you will see a preacher-prophet wrestling with different contexts. The tone of judgment and warning in chapters 1–25 gives way to one of comfort and hope in chapters 26–52.

[3]Peter Steinfels, "Beliefs: In this postmodern world, what religious thinkers may need is a scholarly new postcolonial posting," *The New York Times,* 3 August 2002.

[4]Aristotle, *On Rhetoric: A Theory of Civic Discourse,* trans. George A. Kennedy (New York: Oxford University Press, 1991), 48.

[5]James F. Murphy, *Rhetoric in the Middle Ages: A History of Rhetorical Theory from St. Augustine to the Renaissance* (Berkeley: University of California Press, 1981), 307.

[6]George A. Lindbeck, *The Nature of Doctrine: Religion and Theology in a Postliberal Age* (Philadelphia: The Westminster Press, 1984); Charles L. Campbell, *Preaching Jesus: New Directions for Homiletics in Hans Frei's Postliberal Theology* (Grand Rapids: Eerdmans, 1997).

[7]Lindbeck, *The Nature of Doctrine*, 16–17.
[8]Ibid., 22.
[9]Ibid.
[10]Ibid., 16.
[11]Ibid., 18.
[12]Ibid., 33.
[13]Campbell, *Preaching Jesus*, 33.
[14]Ibid., 64.
[15]Ibid., 69.
[16]Ibid., 216.
[17]Ibid., 158.
[18]Ronald J. Allen, *The Teaching Sermon* (Nashville: Abingdon Press, 1995), 26.
[19]Mary Catherine Hilkert, *Naming Grace: Preaching and the Sacramental Imagination* (New York: Continuum, 1997), 47.
[20]Ibid.
[21]Christine M. Smith, *Preaching as Weeping, Confession, and Resistance* (Louisville: Westminster/John Knox Press, 1992).
[22]Ibid., 5.
[23]Ibid.
[24]John S. McClure, *Other-wise Preaching: A Postmodern Ethic for Homiletics* (St. Louis: Chalice Press, 2001), 19.
[25]Ibid., 17.
[26]Quoted in ibid., 7, from Rebecca Chopp, *The Power to Speak: Feminism, Language, God* (New York: Crossroad, 1991).
[27]McClure, *Other-wise Preaching*, 3.
[28]Ibid.
[29]Ibid., 9.
[30]Ibid., 1.
[31]Graham Ward, *Theology and Contemporary Critical Theory* (London: Macmillan Press, 2000), 117.
[32]Ibid.
[33]Ibid.
[34]Catherine J. C. Pickstock, "Is Orthodoxy Radical?" *Affirming Catholicism*; information obtained from http://www.affirmingcatholicism.org.uk/Aritcle.asp?UID=70 on August 9, 2002.
[35]John Milbank, *Theology and Social Theory* (Oxford, UK: Blackwell, 1990); John Milbank, *The Word Made Strange: Theology, Language, Culture* (Oxford, UK: Blackwell, 1997); Catherine Pickstock, *After Writing: On the Liturgical Consummation of Philosophy* (Oxford, UK: Blackwell, 1998); Graham Ward, *Barth, Derrida and the Language of Theology* (Cambridge, UK: Cambridge University Press, 1995); Graham Ward, *Theology and Contemporary Critical Theory* (London: Macmillan, 1996).
[36]John Milbank, Catherine Pickstock, Graham Ward, eds., *Radical Orthodoxy* (London: Routledge, 1999).
[37]Ibid., 1–2.
[38]Pickstock, "Is Orthodoxy Radical?" 3.
[39]Ibid., 2.
[40]Ibid.
[41]Ibid.
[42]Ibid.
[43]Ibid., 3.
[44]Ibid.
[45]Ibid., 4.
[46]Ibid.
[47]Ibid.
[48]John Milbank, "Knowledge: The Theological Critique of Philosophy in Hamann and Jacobi," in *Radical Orthodoxy*, 24.
[49]Catherine Pickstock, *After Writing*, 121.
[50]Ibid., 253.
[51]Ibid.
[52]Laurence Hull Stookey, *Calendar: Christ's Time for the Church* (Nashville: Abingdon Press, 1996), 33.

Chapter 6: Preaching and the Redemption of Language

[1]T. S. Eliot, *Four Quartets,* The Centenary Edition (New York: Harcourt Brace, 1971), 19.

[2]Maurice Blanchot, *The Writing of the Disaster* (Lincoln, Neb.: University of Nebraska Press, 1995).

[3]Christine Smith, *Preaching as Weeping, Confession, and Resistance: Radical Responses to Radical Evil* (Louisville: Westminster John Knox Press, 1992).

[4]See in particular Walter Brueggemann, *Cadences of Home: Preaching among Exiles* (Louisville: Westminster John Knox Press, 1997).

[5]Ana Maria Rizzuto, *The Birth of the Living God: A Psychoanalytic Study* (Chicago: University of Chicago Press, 1979; Ludwig Binswanger, *Being-in-the-World: Selected papers of Ludwig Binswanger,* trans. and with critical introduction by Jacob Needleman (New York: Basic Books, 1963).

[6]See Rebecca Chopp, *The Power to Speak: Feminism, Language, God* (New York: Crossroad, 1991).

[7]Anna Carter Florence, "Preaching as Testimony, Towards a Women's Preaching Tradition and New Homiletic Models" (Ph.D. diss., Princeton Theological Seminary, 2000), 168.

[8]Henry Mitchell, *The Recovery of Preaching* (San Francisco: Harper and Row, 1977), 37.

[9]Warren H. Stewart, *Interpreting God's Word in Black Preaching* (Valley Forge, Pa.: Judson Press, 1984), 47.

[10]Olin P. Moyd, *The Sacred Art: Preaching and Theology in the African-American Tradition* (Cleveland: Judson Press, 1995), 106.

[11]Blanchot, *The Writing of the Disaster,* 21.

[12]See Emmanuel Levinas, *Otherwise than Being or Beyond Essence,* trans. Alphonso Lingis (The Hague: Martinus Nijhoff Publishers, 1981), 48. This "saying" is, as Levinas puts it, "a signifyingness dealt the other prior to all objectification. It does not consist in giving signs."

[13]See especially Justo González and Catherine González, *Liberation Preaching: The Pulpit and the Oppressed* (Nashville: Abingdon Press, 1980); John S. McClure, *The Roundtable Pulpit: Where Leadership and Preaching Meet* (Nashville: Abingdon Press, 1995); Lucy Atkinson Rose, *Sharing the Word: Preaching in the Roundtable Church* (Louisville: Westminster John Knox Press, 1997); Smith, *Preaching as Weeping;* Kathy Black, *A Healing Homiletic: Preaching and Disability* (Nashville: Abingdon Press, 1996); John S. McClure and Nancy J. Ramsay, *Telling the Truth: Preaching About Sexual and Domestic Violence* (Cleveland: United Church Press, 1998); Florence, "Preaching as Testimony"; Brueggemann, *Cadences of Home;* Chopp, *The Power to Speak;* William E. Dorman and Ronald J. Allen, "Preaching as Hospitality," *Quarterly Review* 14 (1994): 295–310; Ronald J. Allen, *Interpreting the Gospel: An Introduction to Preaching* (St. Louis: Chalice Press, 1998); Sally Brown, "Preaching Ethics Reconsidered: The Social Construction of Christian Moral Reasoning and the Reimagination of Power in Preaching According to the Cross" (Ph.D. diss., Princeton Theological Seminary, 2001); John S. McClure, *Other-wise Preaching: A Postmodern Ethic for Homiletics* (St. Louis: Chalice Press, 2001); L. Susan Bond, *Trouble with Jesus: Women, Christology, and Preaching* (St. Louis: Chalice Press, 1999); Leonora Tubbs Tisdale, *Preaching as Local Theology and Folk Art* (Minneapolis: Fortress Press, 1997); Charles L. Campbell and Stanley P. Saunders, *The Word on the Street: Performing the Scriptures in the Urban Context* (Grand Rapids: Eerdmans, 2000).

Chapter 7: Preaching

[1]Miriam Therese Winter, *God-with-Us: Resources for Prayer and Praise* (Nashville: Abingdon, 1979), 83. Winter is quoting from Anthony Padovano, *Free To Be Faithful* (Paramus, New Jersey: Paulist Press, 1972), 31.

[2]Teresa Ortiz, *Never Again a World Without Us: Voices Of Mayan Women in Chiapas, Mexico* (Washington D.C.: The Ecumenical Program on Central America and the Caribbean, 2001), 99. See Ortiz's entire chap. 3 for a more complete discussion of the Zapastist Movement in Chiapas.

[3]Peggy McIntosh, "White Privilege And Male Privilege: A Personal Account of Coming to See Correspondences Through Work in Women's Studies," in *Race, Class, and Gender: An Anthology,* ed. Margaret L. Andersen and Patricia Hill Collins (Belmont, Calif.: Wadsworth, 1992). McIntosh talks about privilege and critiques some of the ways writers use this term to describe what she would prefer describing as "unearned advantage" and "conferred

dominance." These terms do seem a more truthful description of the actual reality of how unequal power functions and how it is granted.

⁴I discussed this entire section in great detail with Rev. Delle McCormick. She confirmed that what I observed in the worship service in Amatenango are the committed practices of Carlo Celli, Paty Camacho, and the indigenous women and men who are members of this community. With great intention Carlo uses his clerical power minimally, and women in particular are invited and encouraged to participate fully as leaders in their liturgical life.

⁵This is almost a direct quote from Rev. Delle McCormick as she reflected on this particular church in the diocese of San Cristobal de las Casas, and the organizational and religious commitments that have been foundational to the life of this community for more than forty years.

⁶Ortiz, *Never Again a World Without Us*, 174–75. The quote about the "queen being Christ and those who represent Christ in the world" is a quote Rev. McCormick shared with me based on a conversation with a her friend, a member of Las Abejas.

⁷Ibid., chap. 5, for a more complete discussion of the work and struggle of Las Abejas in Chenalhó.

⁸This is only a part of what is actually printed on the sculpture in Acteal. I also have a piece of correspondence from the Danish artist, Jens Galschiot, explaining why he incorporated reptiles and the large snake into the design.

⁹In the "Christian Community Bible, Catholic Pastoral Edition," these Beatitudes would translate or read as "fortunate are those," not "blessed are those." This Bible is published by St. Paul Publications, Makati, Philippines, 1994, translated, presented, and commented on for the Christian communities of the Philippines and the Third World and for those who seek God.

¹⁰The major critique I offer about authority appears in my first book *Weaving the Sermon: Preaching in a Feminist Perspective* (Louisville: Westminster/John Knox Press 1989). Chapter 3, "The Loom of Authority: Mutuality and Solidarity," particularly explores this issue.

¹¹Henry Mitchell, *Black Preaching: The Recovery of a Powerful Art* (Nashville: Abingdon Press, 1990), 21.

¹²I would like to call attention here to Walter Brueggemann's book *Cadences of Home: Preaching Among Exiles* (Louisville: Westminster John Knox Press, 1997), especially the chapter "Testimony as a Decentered Mode of Preaching." I am in disagreement with Brueggemann in his basic assumption that Christians in the United States experience their religious lives as those who are in exile, and thus preachers are "de-centered" from the places of real power in our society. Mainline Christian people and preachers may not share the same kind of power they once did in the United States, and perhaps this is a just thing, not something to lament. Yet, even more importantly, in relation to the rest of the world we are not "de-centered" in the ways I am urging and suggesting throughout this section.

¹³The concept of "re-membering" has been used in feminist/womanist/mujerista theological literature for many years now—so much so, it would be difficult if not impossible to name the first person who used this term as a redemptive term of restoration, repair, and reparation.

¹⁴Even though I am not directly quoting from Sallie McFague's book *The Body of God: An Ecological Theology* (Minneapolis: Fortress Press, 1993), I do want to lift up the importance of her work for urging Christian people to think about the world as "God's body." I am drawing on that image at this point in my reflections and extending the metaphor of the Body to point also to the many "bodies" of religious communities within which preachers preach and engage in ministry.

¹⁵Bill Moyers, *Facing Evil*, videotape (Alexandria, Virginia: PBS Video), no. BMSP-000.

Chapter 8: Keeping in Touch with God

¹Denise Levertov, "Flickering Mind," in *A Door in the Hive* (New York: New Directions, 1989).

²Othmar Keel, *The Symbolism of the Biblical World: Ancient Near Eastern Iconography and The Book of Psalms*, trans. Timothy Hallett (Winona Lake, Ind.: Eisenbrauns, 1997).

³Ibid., 355.

⁴Robert Frost, "The Pasture," in *The Poetry of Robert Frost: The Collected Poems, Complete and Unabridged* (New York: Holt Rinehart & Winston, 1975).

⁵Thomas H. Troeger, "Each Breath Is Borrowed Air," in *Above the Moon Earth Rises* (New York: Oxford University Press, 2002), 8.

⁶"Prayer to Every God," in James B. Pritchard, *Ancient Near Eastern Texts Relating to the Old Testament* (Princeton, N. J.: Princeton University Press, 1969), 391-92.

⁷Ibid.

⁸*The Psalter: A Faithful and Inclusive Rendering from the Hebrew into Contemporary English*, from The International Commission on English in the Liturgy (Liturgy Training Publications, 1994), Psalm 131:2.

Chapter 9: Disrupting a Ruptured World

¹For this translation, see Joel Green, *The Gospel of Luke* (Grand Rapids: Eerdmans, 1997), 210.

²Ibid. 210–11.

³William A. Clebsch and Charles R. Jaekle, *Pastoral Care in Historical Perspective* (New York, London: Jason Aronson, 1983).

⁴See Mary Donovan Turner and Mary Linn Hudson, *Saved from Silence: Finding Women's Voice in Preaching* (St. Louis: Chalice Press, 1999), 54–58.

Chapter 10: Preaching as a Theological Venture

¹Paul Scott Wilson, *Imagination of the Heart: New Understandings in Preaching* (Nashville: Abingdon Press, 1988).

²Martin Luther, "The Freedom of a Christian," in John Dillenberger, *Martin Luther: Selections from His Writings* (Garden City, New York: Anchor Book, Doubleday & Company, Inc., 1961), 65.

³Martin Luther, "Secular Authority: To What Extent It Should Be Obeyed," in John Dillenberger, *Martin Luther: Selections*, 386-87.

⁴Martin Luther, "The Pagan Servitude of the Church," in John Dillenberger, *Martin Luther: Selections,* 346.

⁵Martin Luther, "Sermons on the Catechism," in John Dillenberger, *Martin Luther: Selections,* 227–28.

⁶John Calvin, *Institutes of the Christian Religion,* John T. McNeill, ed., Ford Lewis Battles, trans., vol. 2 (Philadelphia: The Westminster Press, 1960), IV:1:5, 1018.

⁷Ibid.

⁸The literal meaning usually included the metaphorical meaning of a text. One of the last major textbooks in homiletics to use the term *literal meaning* was M. Reu, *Homiletic* (Chicago: Wartburg Publishing House, 1924 [reprinted Grand Rapids: Baker Book House, 1967]), 349–61. The term arose in the first 1500 years of the church when fourfold exegesis was practiced and every text was understood to have four meanings: literal (historical-grammatical); anagogical (eschatological); moral (ethical); and allegorical (theological, centered on Christ).

⁹I have dealt with this subject extensively in Paul Scott Wilson, *God Sense: Reading the Bible for Preaching* (Nashville: Abingdon Press, 2001), from which I derive some of the following argument.

¹⁰Carl E. Bratten and Robert W. Jenson, eds., *Reclaiming the Bible for the Church* (Grand Rapids, Mich., and Cambridge, UK: Eerdmans, 1995), x.

¹¹See Wilson, *God Sense,* 69–71, for a more extensive sampling of questions for theological exegesis.

¹²See Paul Scott Wilson, *The Four Pages of a Sermon: A Guide to Biblical Preaching* (Nashville: Abingdon Press, 1999), 159–61.

¹³Stephen Farris, *Preaching That Matters: The Bible and Our Lives* (Louisville: Westminster John Knox, 1998), 75–124.

¹⁴David L. Bartlett, *Between the Bible and the Church: New Methods for Biblical Preaching* (Nashville: Abingdon Press, 1999), 29.

¹⁵Nancy Lammers Gross, *If You Cannot Preach Like Paul…* (Grand Rapids: Eerdmans, 2002), 12.

¹⁶Ibid., 37.

¹⁷Ibid., 139.

¹⁸Haddon W. Robinson, *Preaching Biblically: The Development and Delivery of Expository Messages* (Grand Rapids: Baker Academic, 2001).

[19]Our conversation was a pedagogy laboratory presentation on "Should We Teach One Method or Several" at the Academy of Homiletics, Eden Seminary, St. Louis, on November 30, 2001.

[20]Ronald J. Allen, *Interpreting the Gospel* (St. Louis: Chalice Press, 1998), 177–206.

[21]Ronald J. Allen, "Notes from my Presentation from the Pedagogy Lab, 'Should We Teach One Method or Several,'" published on the Academy of Homiletics Web site at http://www.homiletics.org

[22]Thomas G. Long, *The Witness of Preaching* (Louisville: Westminster Press/John Knox Press, 1989), 86–91.

[23]Henry H. Mitchell, *Celebration and Experience in Preaching* (Nashville: Abingdon Press, 1990), 52.

[24]David Buttrick, *Homiletic: Moves and Structures* (Philadelphia: Fortress Press, 1987), 23–69.

[25]See Paul Scott Wilson, *The Practice of Preaching* (Nashville: Abingdon Press, 1995), 146–72.

[26]Sandra M. Schneiders, *The Revelatory Text: Interpreting the New Testament as Sacred Scripture* (New York: Harper San Francisco, 1991), 163.